Easy Crafts
FOR THE
INSANE

A
Mostly Funny
Memoir of
Mental Illness and
Making Things

Kelly Williams Brown

G. P. PUTNAM'S SONS
New York

PUTNAM
— EST. 1838 —
G. P. PUTNAM'S SONS
Publishers Since 1838
An imprint of Penguin Random House LLC
penguinrandomhouse.com

Copyright © 2021 by Kelly Williams Brown

Hardcover ISBN: 9780593187784
eBook ISBN: 9780593187791

Printed in the United States of America
1st Printing

Book design by Ashley Tucker

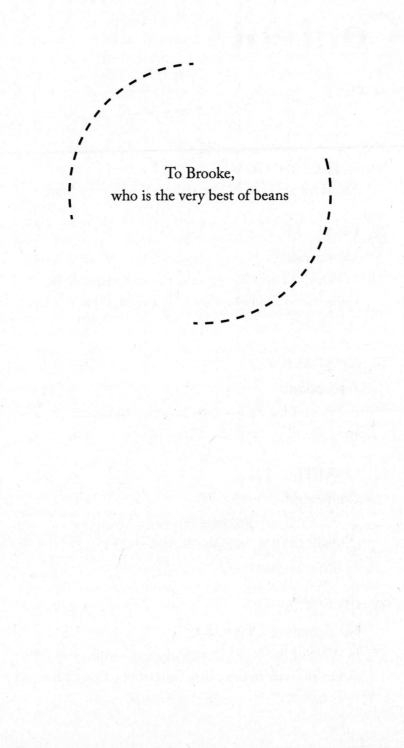

To Brooke,
who is the very best of beans

Contents

"All your sorrows have been
wasted on you if you have not yet
learned how to be wretched."

—Seneca the Younger, *Consolation to Helvia*

Easy Crafts

FOR THE

INSANE

Thank, or at Least Acknowledge, Your Lucky Stars

THERE WAS A TIME WHEN ALL I COULD DO WAS MAKE little paper stars. I was too depressed to do anything else; also, my right arm was broken and my left shoulder was dislocated, which I found limiting.

I guess I was also pretty good at ordering Postmates, lying on my couch, and watching the news in a catatonic state, but none of those resulted in a giant bowl of adorable things.

There is very, very, very, very little fun to be had when neither your arms nor your brain work. But at least I could make stars, and I threw myself into them. I don't know how many little paper stars I made, but certainly thousands. Maybe tens of thousands.

Lucky paper stars, en masse, are like dried beans or sprinkles insofar as they are tremendously satisfying to plunge your hand into. With these, you can do just that without upsetting other bulk-aisle patrons. So I was free to carefully pull the bowl close to my functioning hand, wave my fingers, plunge them in, and watch the little stars ripple and jump.

Even now, years later, evidence of my origami handiwork pops up everywhere in my house. I find little paper stars under the coffee table, caught between the cupboard and the wall, and in random drawers, each one an extremely cute reminder of the worst time of my life.

✂

Thank Your Lucky Stars

This is a frustrating craft—at first! You will make 10 or 15 of these, and they will look wonky and dumb, and you will feel annoyed. It's a steep learning curve, but once you get it, it's super easy, almost reflexive. Commit to making at least 20 (they take fewer than 90 seconds apiece), and you will happily make 20,000.

Also, I know for a fact that you can do this craft with literally no arms (more on that later), so have some perseverance.

Materials:

Long strips of paper. That's it. You can buy them online, at Michaels, or at Japanese stationery stores, or you can just cut them out of magazines. Anything works, as long as it's not super thick. Construction paper won't work; printer paper is good; magazine paper is nearly perfect. Make it about ⅓ inch (1cm) wide by at least 10 inches (25.4cm) long. Sometimes I'll stack a bunch of magazine pages and then use a paper cutter to do a bunch at once. Visually, you'll only see the last 1 or 2 inches (2.5 to 5.1cm) of the strip on the star itself; I find stripes turn out especially cute.

Instructions:

1. Pick up your first strip of paper, holding about 1 inch (2.5cm) from the end, and curl that end behind the main strip to form a little loop. Carefully tuck the end into a simple knot.

2. Slowly and gently tighten the knot by tugging on both ends and jostling the middle until it is nice and tight. Flatten this. The

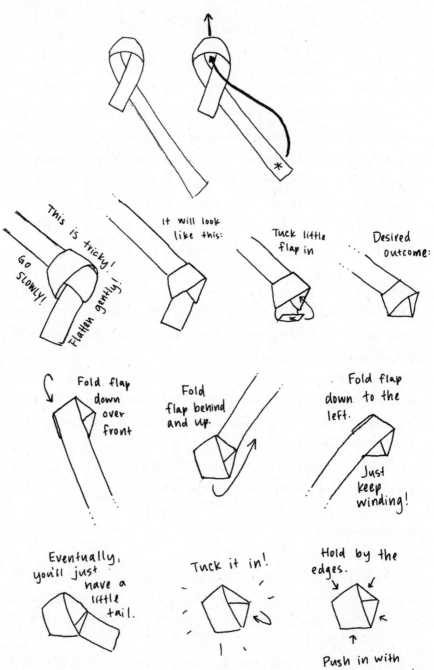

This is tricky!

Go SLOWLY!

Flatten gently!

It will look like this:

Tuck little flap in

Desired outcome:

Fold flap down over front

Fold flap behind and up.

Fold flap down to the left.

Just keep winding!

Eventually, you'll just have a little tail.

Tuck it in!

Hold by the edges.

Push in with your fingernails.

flattened knot makes a five-sided, pentagram shape. Try not to read too much into this.

3. Fold the short end of the paper around the back of your pentagram knot, and tuck it in. Take the long end of the paper and begin to wind it around the pentagram. Follow the angles. When you're almost at the end of the strip, tuck it under the flap. If it feels too long, carefully fold it back on itself and *then* tuck it.

4. Hold the small pentagram *by the edges.* Carefully pinch two sides with your fingernails until it puckers and forms points. Do the same thing on the opposite sides.

5. Hey, look, it's a tiny star! Put it in a bowl. Start another.

If you have it in you, think a small nice thing as you wrap the star into itself. *It will not always be this,* maybe, or *I exist in the same time and space as flamingos; perhaps this is the year I will see one in person.* If things are especially dire, just contemplate Dolly Parton. Remember that if she met you, she would like you. Picture her saying, "Well, haigh! Ahm Dolly! It is SO nice to meet yeeeeew!"

Keep making more stars; keep putting them in the bowl. Put in red ones and brown ones and blue ones and glitter ones. Make them again and again and again, until your fingers can do this without a single thought in your mind. Make them in front of the TV when you need a distraction from your life; make them when you are on hold with the hospital's billing department; make them while you cry. Tell yourself they will bring you luck, if not today or tomorrow then someday. Know that luck is real, and change is real, and tomorrow is going to be a lot better. Or at least different.

✂

Maybe we all, at some point, find ourselves in the middle of a life that we do not recognize. Or maybe it's just me. You go along to get along, you fake it 'til you make it, you follow the steps as you understand them and then, one day, you are the roadrunner off the cliff, still sprinting, supported by nothing but your own conviction that this is what one does. And then you are falling.

Things weren't perfect, of course, but I took pleasure in my life; my friends; my family; my giant precious neurotic angel-dog, Eleanor. I wrote things and went places and saw people. I pored through the aisles of Goodwill to find alarming tchotchkes to hide in my mother's bathroom cabinet. I made happy, involuntary noises when eating prosciutto or burrata.

Then, one by one, my body dissolved, my mind dissolved, my relationships dissolved; the things that anchored me to life slowly faded.

Honestly, I had it coming. I had this ridiculous, picture-perfect five-year run that I knew was just absurd and would not last.

It started with my first book deal, which was akin to being struck by lightning.

I'd worked for years as a newspaper reporter, the only thing I'd ever wanted to do. Everything about being a reporter suited me—go out in the world, see everything, ask any questions you like with that little notebook in your hand lending legitimacy to your curiosity (also: nosiness). I covered events, music, and nightlife, which, in my town meant garage bands, the Oregon State Fair, and alpaca farms during baby alpaca season. I wanted to do that forever, but I couldn't, because the journalism industry I was deeply in love with was dissolving in real time.

So I began to think about what else I could do. I applied for jobs like assistant public information officer at the Department of Sewerage and Waterworks. It didn't have the same ring as "newspaper reporter," but, hey—it had health insurance and perhaps would mean no gutting layoffs every six months.

Then I had an idea for a book full of the practical parts of being a grown-up (getting renters' insurance! asking for a raise! keeping counters clean, which I still never do!). To tie it all together, I made up a really irksome but memorable word that is now mocked on podcasts, emblazoned on hats at Target, and somehow came to embody society's ideas about a whole generation of millennials . . . when really all I was trying to do was share a few handy tips and maybe make rent while local journalism burned around me. A few years later and voilà! I was the "Adulting" girl, an avatar of togetherness and competence, which, again, *I truly never was.*

I will take a moment to apologize for introducing the word *adulting* to the world, which annoyed me even as it came out of my mouth the first time. Now, almost 10 years later, I see it on Instagram and ironic T-shirts and as titles of books that other people have written, and it's still annoying. I don't apologize for the book itself, which I maintain is quite good. The only thing inventing a word gets you is the fun assholery of absolutely insisting to strangers in bars that yes, you made it up—"NO, SERIOUSLY, LOOK IT UP. IT'S ON KNOWYOURMEME.COM."

I was good at gathering information and putting it together in a readable way; I was good at comforting people who are being too hard on themselves and are doing much better than they give themselves credit for. It was not blithe or dishonest. I acknowledged my own flaws and never pretended I was a perfect or even above-average adult.

But everyone thought I was! Somehow I became associated with this persona of perfection, the portrait of having one's shit together that was, decidedly, not me. This was a very effective way to tee myself up for a lifetime of disappointing others with my haplessness.

So, the briefest recap: I got discovered out of nowhere, sold a book at auction that became a bestseller, spoke at NASA, had a beautiful wedding, was the subject of a very kind *New York Times* profile, and became known as an expert on how to be an adult *and* how to be gracious . . . even though I'm not very good at either of those things.

For the first time in my life, I didn't have to check my bank account before I paid my car insurance: *I put that shit on auto-pay!* It was a charmed life, although as a lifelong depressive, this didn't prevent me from sometimes thinking it would be pretty convenient if a semi smashed into me on my way home.

Think of some achievement or honor or item or person that you thought was standing between you and happiness. When you got it, did you find yourself whole and happy? Or temporarily satisfied but then hungry for the next thing?

I was finding success hollow. It is amazing, yes, and it was fun in the moment and made for an impressive bio. But it doesn't—and can't—sustain you. The quality of your relationships, the skill of building and keeping contentment, and your ability to sit with pain and not squirm away from it is what will *actually* keep you going after that first flush of happiness. Not that I understood any of this back then. Creating a life on the memory of something that, even in the moment, you didn't think you deserved is not a stable foundation.

And then, the foundation crumbled further. I got a divorce, a certain someone was elected president, my antidepressant stopped working, my body started breaking, and my luck ran out. Life began to rapidly dissolve. All I had left to sustain me was the small, joyous triumph of making things. Like those little paper stars that took almost zero brainpower but somehow kept me moving, doing, *creating* during the moments when everything (and everyone) else abandoned me.

Crafting, in fact, got me through a pretty terrible 700 days. I was such a wretch during this period, I cannot even tell you. Things went from bad to worse, from worse to atrocious, and from atrocious to unthinkable, at which point the whole thing just became bleakly hilarious. Sadly, I was too depressed to appreciate jokes, even really good ones, like what my life had become.

I'll tell you about most of them in here, but some highlights include:

- Breaking three of my four limbs in *separate* and *unrelated* incidents;

- Cat and grandmother deaths within a week of each other;

- What a therapist accurately billed as "catastrophic loss of chosen family";

- Sinking into a deep depression that meant I wrote (and did) nothing for a year;

- Four days of in-patient mental health treatment, which I like to call my "rest cure" because in my mind I am a fancy Victorian lady;

- A relationship's irreparable breakdown within 36 hours of breaking my ankle;

- Dad-cancer; and

- Trump.

As you can imagine, it was *quite the time!*

Seeking help and being open about what was going on was complicated by my career, which, as noted, consisted of giving helpful advice to people who feel sad and confused. I was—other people seemed to think—someone with ideas on how to live one's best life, ideas that didn't include lying listlessly on a dog-hair-covered couch watching *Bob's Burgers* on repeat for months at a time.

"Didn't you write a *book* on this?" someone says when I make any sort of error, which is often, as I'm a space cadet with poor short-term memory and executive function.

"You did! You did write a book on this!" Depression whispers malevolently. "Why in God's name would anyone want to listen to you? How do you feel about your work and success being built upon a lie? Is that a caramel wrapper in your hair? What percentage, by weight, of this couch is dog hair? Why is the coffee table sticky? Were you thinking, when you bought this robe, that it was going to become your primary garment?"

This is all a very unhealthy and not-at-all-useful outlook that, with time and medication and effort, has improved somewhat.

I'm not alone in this. Well, I'm alone in the specifics of

these 700 days, which, taken cumulatively, make it seem like I was cursed by a mean elf who specializes in plaguing middle-class white women in their 30s. But I'm not alone in some things.

My brain sometimes doesn't make the right chemicals in the right amount—an ongoing problem for 20 years now. If it were, say, my kidney doing this, I could explain, "Hey! Got a wonky kidney, here, but I'm working on it. Please still invite me to stuff, and if I'm feeling good, I'll be there!" and people would get it. Maybe they would also know that sometimes I am not present because I'm exhausted and/or scared, and that I didn't text back because it felt like the equivalent of climbing a mountain, somehow. But it's my brain, not my kidney, and so the very dull fact that it's *that* organ improperly functioning becomes this huuuuuuge thing that I'm not allowed/too ashamed to talk about, even though it affects so much.

I so, so often have felt like I am too much, exhausting even to myself, and doing everything in the wrong amount. Eating too much or too little, drinking too much or too little, or feeling things too much or too little.

It is so easy to feel lonely and adrift a lot of the time. This is going to be a weird digression, but please come with me: Are you familiar with Caroline Manzo, formerly a Real Housewife of New Jersey? I think I am most jealous, of all the people in the world, of Caroline. She has this enormous clan of an extended family that is constantly gathering to eat thousands of dollars' worth of meat together. She knows in her heart there is no better place in the world for her than Franklin Lakes, New Jersey, where she can sit and gaze proudly upon the world she has created.*

More than anything, Caroline has *certainty*—about how life is

---

* This world, it should be said, is not perfect, and I am not suggesting one follow Caroline in all ways. Google can tell you more about this if you are curious.

and how life is supposed to be, about herself, and about her place in the universe. She is so tethered. It's the same envy I feel for the very religious. They don't have to question; they just *know*, and they have hundreds of other people who *also* know, and they're all making something delicious for this Sunday's potluck. The idea of this obedience and submission is chafing, but it sure does look nice. I wish I knew.

But honestly, in this case, I'm not sure how it could've been helped. A bunch of bad things happened, one after another. Each time something bad happened, I withdrew from the world a little bit more and cared about my life a little bit less. It's always been the case that sometimes I don't feel like being alive, in the same way that I sometimes don't feel like vacuuming my house or following through on happy-hour plans, but it had never been like this.

I had all kinds of resources at my disposal, and I still couldn't get the help I needed. With great and extended effort, I finally found it, but I had to almost die for that to happen.

But before I had *help*-help, I had crafts. Crafting has always calmed me, made me feel better, and given my hands something to do so my brain can stop shrieking at me for one gosh darn second.

So in those 700 days, when I wasn't able to work, leave my house, or function as a human, I crafted. I couldn't write—I didn't have anything to say, plus one doesn't get much writing done when one is in bed 14 hours a day and catatonically watching MSNBC the other 10—but I could embroider, letter, teach myself block printing, cut out Bad Decision Shrinky Dink charm bracelets, make weird modular origami spheres, fold literally thousands of tiny stars, and, just for good measure, make those trivets out of plastic tube-shaped beads that you then iron to melt one side.

Crafting gives me a sense of accomplishment even when I feel like I can't accomplish anything. Crafting is tangible proof that I can do *something*. To craft is to set things correct in tiny ways—to make this crease or that stitch or move that candle over a bit because it just looks *better* there—and I can almost always effect these changes in the universe. Crafting reminds me that my brain moving differently from other people's brains is not all a bad thing.

Once, I was talking to (or, more accurately, crying on the phone with probably also) Carol, one of my mom's best friends. Carol is an incredible artist and said something that made me feel so much better.

Tenderness, she said, is the price of being an artist. If you want to see and create things that other humans haven't seen or created, that means you're going to feel things a little bit more than others do. Those two parts of oneself cannot be divorced. The pain is both a feature and a bug.

If you think about it, it's a little absurd that we get depressed, on an evolutionary level. Experiencing something that makes us 1) stop taking care of ourselves, 2) uninterested in sex, and 3) not eat properly because we're too busy sleeping 20 hours a day doesn't make a ton of evolutionary sense. But it's so, so common—the number one disability in the world—and something experienced by 30 to 50 percent of Americans at some point in their lives. So, the theory goes, it must do *something*.

Some theorize that depression is, in fact, an adaptation because the depressed are really, really good at dwelling on things. We have "depressive ruminations," as Paul W. Andrews and J. Anderson Thomson Jr. put it, and "this thinking style is often highly analytical. They dwell on a complex problem, breaking it down into smaller components, which are considered one at a time."*

Because, they said, you're not concerning yourself with things like other humans or basic hygiene, you can truly lean in to solving whatever problem has swallowed you whole.

As someone who has always wanted a normie brain, this brings me comfort, in the same way learning that being a night owl doesn't mean you're a lazy dirtbag. It was evolutionarily useful to have a few humans who are wide awake at 1 a.m. to watch over things and, for whatever reason, it is useful for humanity to include depressed people who are great at dwelling on shit.

These days, I'm feeling a *lot* better, thanks to lots of things that are part of that invisible work I mentioned, and also—perhaps mainly!—that I was finally able to access care. Most days, I feel pretty, or even really, good. I am not resentful that I have to leave my bed in the morning. I am happy when good things happen and sad when sad things happen, in reasonable amounts. As my therapist once pointed out, we don't really have bad days, we have bad hours or moments.

---

* Paul W. Andrews and J. Anderson Thomson Jr., "The Bright Side of Being Blue: Depression as an Adaptation for Analyzing Complex Problems."

But sometimes, ugly stuff bubbles up, so it's nice that I can always just go make some crafts.

I cannot soothe my mind once and have it be done. I have not and will not permanently cure myself, in these pages or otherwise. No amount of peppy self-talk cures diabetes or hypertension, and I'm done pretending this is different. The brain is not special and apart; it's cells, chemicals, and electricity that function (or don't) for reasons that we will likely never fully understand.*

There's this temptation, in books about mental health (or heartbreak or addiction or any of the awful things that happen to us, although often with our enthusiastic help), to wrap everything up. I *was* drunk, but *now* I'm sober. I *was* depressed, but *now* I'm a sunny little person. That guy *broke my heart*, but the end of that relationship made space for my *one true love*, and so on.

It would be great (both narratively and, um, for my life) if there were some fixed finish line. And I had crossed it. And now I was Better, Forever, and You Could Be, Too. This is not the nature of anything, though. There is not a beginning, a middle, and an end. It's a constant coaxing, reinforced with boundaries and medication. It is following good mental health hygiene—which is the *real* self-care, although it's so, so boring! It is cultivating contentment rather than chasing happiness.

It is patiently asking myself the same questions: "Can you do anything about this right now? Should you do anything about this right now?" It is reciting the same reminders: "You sound really

---

* Seriously! Take, for example, lithium, which is a first-line treatment for bipolar disorder, more than 150 years after we started using it. It's a very simple element, number 3 on the periodic table, with three protons and three electrons . . . and yet it somehow can help with an extremely complicated set of behaviors and symptoms. Why? Well, that's the funny thing: no one knows. In fact, that's the case with many psychiatric drugs. We're not sure *why* they work; they just do.

afraid right now, and that's okay, but I don't think there is any-thing actively dangerous happening." It's accepting that I will sometimes just feel afraid or sad or nothing at all, which is perhaps the worst of the three.

I cannot control the world, and I often cannot control my own mind, but dang it, *I can make you an extremely thoughtful embroidered gift*. No matter how far gone I feel, my fingers still know how to fold an eensy paper star or a cute snail. In this teeny arena, I will always find success, which reminds me of some important things.

I am resilient and scrappy as fuck, and you should never, ever bet against me. My crafts are not perfect or beautiful, but they are charming and I *mean* them. And sometimes, isn't that all one can ask for?

✂

Before we get into it, a brief Q&A.

Q: So, what is this book, exactly?
This book is a bunch of stories about shitty things that happened to me—and shitty things that I did! (funny how those two often coincide)—paired with crafts from those periods, because crafting makes me, and, I think, a lot of people, feel better. So this book is truly a one-stop shop, if your needs are: 1) reading about mental illness, 2) hearing about the time I didn't have any arms, and 3) knowing how to make Shrinky Dink charm bracelets.

Q: Are you good at crafts?
Nope! I mean, I'm an adequate crafter, I guess, but what I lack in skill I make up for in *vast* output. I don't tend toward crafts that require a lot of precision or patience or ability to count carefully

(there are zero sewing, knitting, or lace-making tutorials in this book), which gives my craft tutorials a very accessible vibe. My finished product also has a very "accessible vibe," which is to say they're kind of ratty, but people like them anyway. These are not Martha Stewart–level or even Amy Sedaris–level crafts. This book contains an odd, idiosyncratic collection of the things I've been able to teach myself over the years. To be fair, this could be said of literally every human's creative output.

Q: Why did you use the word *insane*? I don't like that word.
Yeah, I know a lot of people don't. I like it because it's dramatic and old-fashioned and just sort of fun to say or proclaim about yourself. "I'm afraid I was *quite insane*, Theodore!" I say as I recline on a divan, absent-mindedly stroking loose rubies. "I was simply out of my *mind* and hadn't the *slightest* idea how I would ever find it again." Theodore smiles knowingly. He's gay, but somehow also wants to fuck me, and I am deeply grateful for Theodore.

I'm writing this book because there's still a giant stigma around mental health, which—wcird! We managed to make it okay to admit you were pregnant or had cancer or were gay or were any of a million other anodyne human conditions, so hopefully this whole thing is next. But I'm also using that word because this is the water I swim in. I almost died, and I have earned the right to use it. I promise I'm on your team here; I just find pleasure in the word, and there's not that much pleasure to be had in mental illness.

Q: Don't you know that in the grand scheme of things, you're super privileged? Are these real problems?
Yes, I am, and yes, they are. I am insanely lucky, but not in this arena. We live in times of despair and, if these two years taught

me nothing else, they taught me how to be wretched, how to continue moving forward, even, and especially when it feels like there is absolutely nothing to be gained in doing so. And there are so, so many of us who are doing that every day, all the time.

This book is not about, like, the triumph of the human spirit in the wake of genocide. This is about some shitty but also normal human stuff I got through, and how I did it, and also how to make comics about a skeleton version of your mother.

Q: What sorts of anecdotes can I expect in the pages ahead?
I mentioned a lot of it already in the intro, but there's also some Hurricane Katrina stuff, some funny anecdotes from when I was a reporter, and some not-super-funny but also in-no-way-majorly-traumatizing-or-triggering childhood stories. Nothing too wild; mostly what you would expect.

Q: What kinds of crafts?
It's a weird smattering! My table is very, very big when it comes to crafts. There's lettering and a fair amount of origami, which is something I've been very into since 1994. There's watercolors and these fake dragon eggs made of egg-shaped foam and 900 thumb-tacks. They are very heavy and satisfying to click your fingernails against or put directly on your face if you, like me, enjoy exploring a texture that way. These are great for that. Also, small doodles of inconsequential things. If you're legitimately looking to become a serious crafter, this should not be your first stop.

Q: So this is . . . a craft book? A memoir? What are we talking here?
I don't know! I wanted to talk about how I have come to be con-

tent in my own skin, I wanted to
talk about hilarious and awful
things that happened, and I
wanted to talk about down-
strokes versus upstrokes in
calligraphy. I wanted to
talk about dissolving and
having to reconstitute
yourself. And if you can't
reconstitute, if for now you
are just a cup of dirty paintbrush water, that's okay, too.

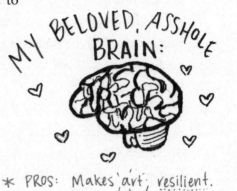

MY BELOVED, ASSHOLE BRAIN:

* PROS: Makes art; resilient.
* CONS: Stops working sometimes.

Every single watercolor you've ever looked at has involved lots and
lots and lots of dirty paintbrush water.

General Crafting Supplies

Crafting, in many cases, isn't the cheapest hobby to start, and I in
no way want to suggest you should bankrupt yourself getting
started. You can always buy more supplies later, if you're into it.

Don't feel like you need to get every single little individual-
ized tool, either. Here's a list of things that are reasonably cheap
and you can use in a variety of ways. Individual projects have
material lists, but these are things that are nice to have on hand
for any number of projects. These recommendations are just my
personal experience, so your mileage may vary (but it probably
won't!).

1. **Pencils in a number of hardnesses:** Great news on pricing—
   pencils are somehow always, like, $1.43 when bought loose. I

get the cheapest version, which is good enough for the girls I go with.* Anyway, go for a 9H (or 8H, 7H, or 6H), which is very hard, for light sketching, and a couple soft ones (7B, 8B, or 9B) for dark lines. Go to an art store and test them on the little pad provided.

2. **A STAEDTLER Mars plastic eraser:** These are white, less than $2, and the best eraser out there. They do create a billion little eraser debris whisps, so be prepared to sweep those up afterward if you're feeling high functioning, or blow hard and let them go all over your floor if you're not.

3. **A white gel pen:** I use a uni-ball brand pen, but honestly, you're already at the art store for the pencils and erasers, and the pens are right there. Test 'em to find one you like!

4. **A mini light tablet:** For *years*, I was constantly annoyed that I didn't have the space or money for a light table, and also that I wasn't a free-spirited loft-living artist in early '90s NYC who of course would have one. But one upside of our hellish-yet-convenient era is that light tablets can be had for $17 on a certain giant online retailer. I use mine for tracing a pattern onto fabric for embroidery, reversed lettering/designs on the flip side of a sheet of paper for linocut prints, over a pencil doodle in pen—

---

* My ex-husband used to say that all the time about, say, a disappointing Trader Joe's frozen burrito. Jesus, he was funny.

the list goes on and on! Also, look, it's entirely possible I've used mine as a thin, perfectly sized TV tray, although how would you know? You weren't even there! Like I said, many uses.

5. **Masking tape:** You need to be able to affix things to your light tablet! And other places! The best way to do this is with a thin roll of masking tape, which releases easily (read: no residue unless you press *really* hard or leave it on for days). You can do a ton of things with it, too: it's a really easy way to label things, and if you've ever marked directly on the wall where you are going to drill a hole, next time put down a strip of masking tape and mark *that*.

6. **Washi tape of choice:** Don't go crazy here. Pick a couple colors or patterns that you like. I go for gold because I want *everything* to be gold. Spray painting things gold is one of my best coping mechanisms. It reminds me that my things are *mine*, and while I cannot and should not control other people, I can definitely gild any inanimate possession I please. This is a very Catholic (and ineffective) solution, but that's never stopped me.

7. **Mod Podge:** The Scottie Pippen of the craft world, Mod Podge can bind almost any porous surface (read: paper, fabric, cardboard, unfinished wood . . .) to itself or another porous surface, and it dries clear. It is perfect for decoupage or sealing acrylic paintings. **Hot tip:** A good way to prevent wrinkles is to spread a thin layer of glue on the back of your paper, let that dry, and then glue down as normal. Also, if you want something to have a matte finish, only make the top coat matte. Otherwise, everything will look cloudy.

8. **E6000:** For when you need something a bit more . . . intense . . . than Mod Podge and/or when you need to glue nonporous surfaces like rhinestones or buttons. Most people would use a hot glue gun instead, but the reasons I don't are deeply personal. I'm always burning myself, and I *hate* the stringiness. It reminds me of pumpkin innards, which are the grossest thing we're expected to touch. If you have a glue gun and you like it, stick with that.

9. **A pack of printer paper:** You'll use it!

10. **An 8.5 × 11-inch hardcover sketchbook:** I use mine for taking notes at work, then practicing my lettering, then doodling, then back to work notes. The key is to leave three pages at the beginning for a table of contents, then number the pages, which makes finding what you're looking for much easier.

11. **Fudenosuke Brush Pen (Hard Tip):** These are the best ones I've used. The tip is very thin and very firm, so you can easily control the thickness when lettering or illustrating. As the name implies, these are Japanese, so you'll probably have to buy them online. The 10-pack is very reasonably priced, although I would recommend buying just one and seeing how you feel before going all-in. The Japanese version of the Pentel Sign Pen with Brush Tip is also great, and it's good for doing slightly larger lettering. The Japanese live in the year 3000 when it comes to pens.

12. Twine and/or fishing line: Lots of things need to be tied! Go for fishing line if you want an invisible option (which, usually you do), or cute twine, perhaps the red-and-white-striped one that makes items bear at least a passing resemblance to a pastry box.

CHAPTER 1

Unmarried

In Which I Leave My Spouse; Flee to Independence, Oregon; and Assume a Future So Bright, Protective Eyewear Is Required

IT WAS THE SUMMER OF 2016, AND I WAS THE MANIFESTA-tion of a 1990s country song about how cool it is to be a gal. My freedom and self-sufficiency oozed from every pore. I felt more powerful and in control of my life than ever before, I was excited about the future, I was bopping around in a 1994 Mazda Miata, and it was *great*.

I'd ejected from my marriage after only a few months, leaving behind a brilliant, loving, and impossible man. I fled to Independence, Oregon (*get it?!?*), population 8,590. I know I am in

THIS WAS ACTUALLY THE VIEW FROM MY WINDOW.

INDEPENDENCE, OREGON

IF IT HAPPENED IN A MOVIE I'D ROLL MY EYES.

INDEPENDENCE because it says that on the water tower right outside my window and also because I am living a romantic comedy with zero subtlety.

I feel an overwhelming sense of freedom that I escaped something I thought inescapable. I am terribly sad, but there is also relief. And, of course, tremendous shame. I got married even though I knew I shouldn't, and I hadn't even made it to our paper anniversary.

"Why did you marry him?" you might ask. Easy: he was the smartest, funniest, and kindest person I'd ever met. All three, by a long shot. He would casually drop things in conversation that rearranged my understanding of the universe. He was, and is, astonishingly loyal and loving. He's a man in his 30s who makes new friends and then keeps them forever, along with dozens of other friends he's made starting from when he was five. He loves, fiercely and loyally, the shit out of people, even—and perhaps especially—when they can't love themselves. His table is big; whenever we went anywhere, he had a bunch of people to see. And all those people were amazing, too.

Before we met, he would save up money and then go on, say, a four-month trip by train. He had been everywhere. He's the best storyteller I've ever known—when I heard him recount a story, even if I had been there, it was changed, becoming hilarious and true in ways I hadn't seen. I loved living in the world of his stories. He made me laugh so, so hard, every day, every hour. I would think of his jokes days later and laugh again. I still do.

We were hanging out at his apartment early on, and somehow farting came up. I tossed off a dumb joke I'd made to every guy I've dated since I was 19 to the effect that although farting was fine for *other* people, I myself had never done it.

"Yeah, no, me either," he said, and then frowned, looking worried. "I mean, what do you think it feels like? Do you think it *hurts*?"

This happened in 2012, and I still sometimes remember it and laugh.

On our first date, I told one of my Amusing Anecdotes™ that I had probably told a dozen times. It was about the first time I was out on assignment with one of my Mississippi coworkers who I will call Don, a charming and insane photographer in his 50s. As soon as we were on the highway, Don, with no prompting, launched into a story about the time he was caught trafficking 50 pounds of weed through rural Mississippi in the '70s. I won't relay the whole roundabout tale here, but the punchline was, "Then the biker said, 'Oh, yeah, that state trooper? That's my brother-in-law. I was *testin'* yew.'"

Former Husband laughed and then said, "And, you know, it's funny because of course that story was also *his* way of testing *you*." I almost fell off my stool. No one else had noticed this thing or arrived at this analysis, not even close.

It was a pattern that would repeat itself again and again. A spoonful weighed a ton. He was smarter and infinitely better-read than me, which of course was hideously annoying, but mostly I could only marvel at his brain—it was just so *fast*. When I was around him, the charisma got all over me—I was funnier, somehow, quicker and cleverer. He made me laugh until I peed, and in return, he told me I was the funniest woman he'd ever met, which goes a long way with me.

No matter how much I seemed to upset him, I knew he saw me in a way that no one else ever had and that he loved what he saw—the good, bad, and ugly. He wrote song after song about me, not uniformly flattering but all exceptionally loving.

One time, I was wandering around in my underwear, and he looked up.

"Jesus fucking Christ, this is ridiculous. You look like . . . like . . . a painting of a really hot woman, or a drawing in a comic book done by someone who actually *likes* women."

I have a gap in my front teeth that I've always been sensitive about—as in, there were large swaths of my life when I thought *I would be cute if it wasn't for that gap.* I have a terribly awkward smile because I spent the first 25 years of my life making sure my lips were firmly closed. At one point I looked into closing the gap.* He was aghast.

"Why would you want to look *more* like everyone in the world?"

So, then, what was the problem?

Well.

As you read the following, please know that I have my side of the story and he has his, and there is no way I could fairly and accurately impart both of them. And that I did love him, and do love him, and wouldn't take back any of it. I would, in fact, give a fairly

---

*This would not have worked because I have what's known as a "persistent gap." Closing it would require oral surgery *and* bolting my teeth together, and at a certain point it's like, eh, clearly this gap is just a part of the deal. Please stop sending me mean emails about it.

glowing letter of recommendation to anyone who wanted to marry him who is not me.

We could not get along for a week to save our goddamn lives. Everything—*everything!*—had to be a fight. I am quite conflict-averse and had never really fought with a significant other before. So imagine my surprise when he got mad at me on our third date, which I was terribly late for. In my defense, I tried to cancel, saying my day had filled up and I couldn't get up to Portland in time, but he said that he'd looked forward to and planned our date, insisted I be there and did not want to reschedule.

When I did finally arrive, he wasn't at his apartment but at a coffee shop nearby, tutoring one of his friends in math. He told me coldly that I could wait until he was done, and so I did, sitting chastised and quiet a few tables away. I'd apologized several times already, starting with when I tried to reschedule, but it still took another one before he looked me in the eyes and told me he forgave me.

I won't lie: this dynamic was new to me, and I interpreted it *not* as someone with an, ahem, rigid belief system who might not always consider my point of view, but rather as someone who "respected himself." Or maybe both were true?

He had an endless appetite for what he always framed as debate . . . but was often extremely stressful for me. I did not share his love of verbal sparring, and I withdrew. When something was wrong between us (always), I imagined myself folding inward, becoming a small, smooth stone, going to a place where whatever bullshit we were on about now couldn't affect me. I appeased and said whatever insincere thing I thought would end the argument. Feel free to place a bet on whether this made things better or worse.

I tried, in my unhealthy way, to put an end to our ongoing discord. I twisted and turned and contorted and moved as quietly as I could, but it seemed that no matter what I did, I always upset him, with words or actions or inaction, in ways that I could not predict. I couldn't be someone who conducted herself in a manner he found acceptable, who didn't warrant constant criticism.

Eventually, I realized this person just didn't exist. Or maybe she did, but I sure as hell wasn't her. At some point, I apparently decided I might as well be dramatically *not* her. If you don't like me when I'm trying, *hoooo boy*, wait until you see what I do when I am entirely out of fucks.

In the grand tradition of misery, I did not keep it to myself but was generous enough to spread my unhappiness around. I drank four or five glasses of wine a night because at that level of drunk, you can pretend a lot of things are okay, and the next day you can lament your hangover instead of where your choices have brought you.

I withheld love and avoided him. The more he ran toward me, the more I desperately wanted to bolt. We were the couple who stressed out others by being constantly tense around each other. I resented it and tried to paper over everything rather than actually solve our problems.

Something neat about staying in a decaying relationship is your slow but notable transformation into a version of yourself who is unrecognizable. This person is so different from who you imagine yourself to be, and yet she looks, talks, and cries just like you. *When did you get so angry?*

I decided perhaps one didn't get to be happy in their relationship, that fighting all the time, about *everything*, was something I needed to be more Zen about. Some people are tall, some people are extremely good at billiards, and some people find life much easier and more calming when they are on the other side of the country from their significant other. Variety: the spice of life!

And like I said a few pages earlier, I *loved* him. And he *loved* me. He was unlike anyone I'd ever met before, and as excruciating as life with him was, life without him felt like it would be worse. He made me feel incredibly safe. He was protective, loyal, and caring, and the same scrappiness that made me crazy at home meant that he moved through life true to his principles and unafraid. I truly *admired* him—he took me to new ideas, new ways to look at the world, and new ways to be. But despite all this, we could not get along.

The way to solve these problems? Yep! Get married.

I am a serial monogamist and had, before he arrived, bailed on several great boyfriends who were marriage material. Why did I always feel the urge to bolt when they wanted to settle down? The commonality in my relationships was me; therefore, perhaps, *I* was the problem. Maybe I was the one incapable of accurately assessing my own relationships and should, instead, outsource this job to the general community. My friends loved him; in fact, we had lots of people in common even before we dated, all of whom were delighted by our pairing.

It felt like I *should* get married, and I was on the wrong side of 30. According to some of my Louisiana college sorority friends, I was on the wrong side of 25. And—this doesn't make me proud— like so many middle-class '90s children, I grew up thinking there was a sensible and obvious order to life. If you followed it, you would be okay. I'd already checked the college and career boxes, so now it was time to check marriage and children.

If anyone reading this is engaged and terrified and constantly doubting yourself, *don't do it*. I know how easy this is to say and how impossible it is to act upon. But seriously and truly, you do not have to get married. That shit is fucking *optional*.

Any engagement, however conflicted, feels like a huge ball rolling fast, its mass composed of family's and friends' expectations and travel plans and deposits and caterers and the fact that you have made this giant, public announcement and everyone liked it on Instagram and it's hard to break up even when you're *not* engaged, and, and, and, and, . . . forever. There might be 14 million external reasons why you should get married. But what if the only reason you shouldn't is inside you? And what if you aren't sure you can trust yourself?

So here, now, is my promise to you: If any of you ever need to leave someone, even the day of, even at the altar, and you are within 50 miles of Salem, Oregon, just email me—pleasesaveme@kelly williamsbrown.com. I will come to you like a falcon to the falconer and swoop you away and we can go get smoothies. If I don't reply in a timely manner (which I almost certainly will not), or the logistics don't work, call an older female friend or relative who has left a bad marriage, and they will be there in 10 seconds. If you're wondering if you *have* to do it, you almost certainly shouldn't.

Yes, the wedding was beautiful—but oh, the internal screaming. A good bit of ugly-crying during our honeymoon in Sicily when, yet again, I'd violated some principle that I didn't understand and he stormed off, leaving me in the street. (This happened several times.) You can go around the world together and still feel alone.

I had a series of increasingly deranged thoughts:

My grandmother didn't have a super-happy marriage, but she was an exceptionally happy person. Maybe I need to meditate more.

The subject of this first-person New York Times *essay felt like she'd made a mistake, too, but through perseverance and personal effort, it turns out that she absolutely did not make a mistake and is now the happiest woman on Earth. Perhaps I am her!*

Maybe I can have some kids and then co-parent with him.
Maybe I will turn into a bird and fly away.

It was utterly impossible to be together in a way that didn't involve constant, grinding conflict. I'm not going to say it was trench warfare, both of us putting everything on the line to gain a yard or two, but . . . it wasn't *not* that.

In the end, there just wasn't a moment when I could acknowledge and act upon the sad, deep truth of our relationship: no matter how much we truly and sincerely loved each other, we were fundamentally very different people, neither of whom could—or should—change enough to satisfy the other.

So, after one especially terrible night, I left.

I fled our house for Salem, my quasi-hometown 45 miles to the south. I said it was because of a book deadline and that I wanted to get away from distractions, but the truth is that I wanted to get away from him. The absence of my husband was deeply soothing.

At some point, a much older friend said to me, "Well, you could divorce. Not everything works out," and this felt like someone saying, "Hey! You actually don't have to eat any more of those burning coals. Stop picking them up and putting them in your mouth. Just *not*-eat them." It was a *revelation.*

Maybe an hour after she said that to me, I was sitting in my friend Emily's backyard. I'd sent a text, and my three closest friends—Emily, Carrie, and Margaret*—dropped everything, Margaret even driving an hour, to sit around a fire with me, do Tarot, and give me space to voice what I'd known for a long time but never said aloud.

"I don't think I can stay married," I said. There was a long pause.

---

* These are not their real names. With very, very few exceptions, no one's real name is being used in this book, and I've changed lots of details. Also, I do not go through life with a tape recorder, so conversations are based on my and other's recollections.

". . . That's a bummer," said Margaret, which was the most perfect thing anyone could've said at that moment.

During our final marriage counseling session, he asked if I loved him. I told him, honestly, that I did love him, deeply, but also affection and patience had slowly dripped out of me. Sometimes you open a drawer and, to your astonishment, it is completely empty.

><

Setting a land-speed record for bailing out of a marriage was never something I anticipated doing. It was, in fact, something that I sanctimoniously imagined *not* doing.

Oh, how I had delighted in predicting, sleuthing, and then judging the divorces of others via social media! It had only been, what, *two* years since they made that big damn deal about everything? There was one especially egregious example with a woman who was actually always very nice to me but was also a Popular Girl and, thus, ripe for my scathing critiques. How dare she have a wedding in front of 500 people, divorce, and then *have another one with the same bridal party!* For the record, her marriage lasted at least twice as long as mine did.

I polished what to say to people who asked how married life is treating me, telling them that unfortunately I did not take to wifeliness, and in fact, divorcée was the role I was born to play! I laughed, and then they laughed, and whatever, it's fine, I'm a melodramatic redhead. I framed the demise of my marriage as an inevitable plot point, and everyone was polite enough to play along.

Hey, ho, it's a funny old life because I was, *right at that very moment,* finishing a book on etiquette called *Gracious.* Like *Adult-*

ing, this was a book made of interviews with people who know things I don't. In this case, I was talking to the most gracious women possible. I'd sit down and ask them how to be kind, how to be patient, how to be a good host, and how to be a loving friend. I'd talk to exquisite, perfect 72-year-olds, women who had conducted their lives with integrity and grace, and try to distill what they'd done. Then, I'd get in my car and cry at how badly I was failing at it.

My crafting tendencies had really blossomed during our engagement and leading up to the wedding. There are so many wedding-themed crafts to distract a reluctant bride. Elaborate personalized favors! Necklaces for your wedding party! Signage! But the craft I delved into most deeply was calligraphy, which, as any newly married person can tell you, comes in handy when it's time to send those darn thank-you notes.

By this point in our marriage, I had sent most, but not all, of our wedding thank-yous (it hadn't yet been a year since we were married, remember, so I was well within my etiquette-approved timeline), using my best calligraphy to fill the front of the envelopes with flourishes and creative spacing. The secret to amazing hand-lettering is that you always put the most effort into the name. Everyone's favorite word is their name, so that's the focal point. Make it big, big, *BIG*. It says, *You. You* are a person I so hoped could be here; *you* are the person who has given us such a wonderfully thoughtful gift.

This can seem insincere unless you get yourself in a headspace where this is true. It's not hard—imagine everything this person went through to give you this gift. (In my thought exercise, we're living in a pre-internet-shopping world . . . go with it.) Just think of how much effort it takes you to get out of bed, much less put on nice clothes and decide you're going out shopping. A lot, right?

(Or is that just me?) Now, think about this person who gave you this gift, to whom you're writing this thank-you note. Picture them in a store, thinking of what would make *you* most happy. Think about them walking up and down the aisles, shaking their head at a few options before finding the perfect item for you. Think about the Netflix shows they could've watched instead if they'd stayed home under a warm blanket. It's a goddamn miracle anyone does anything for us.

ILL-FATED THANK-YOU Cards

So I relished every wedding gift we'd received, and I took my darn time writing out each hand-lettered thank-you note. But, as I was finding, this fanciful envelope scheme was not a great plan. While my recipients loved my calligraphy, the postal sorting machines did not. A few, but not most, of my notes were returned for some odd postal reason. Furthermore, an untold number of those were not returned to me but, rather, showed up at former addresses of mine. This created an ambiguity that haunts me to this day. Did they get my note? And what does one say in a maybe–second round of thank-yous, sent as my marriage is disintegrating before my eyes?

Dear distant relation of my soon-to-be-ex-husband,

It was so lovely to finally meet you! I have heard so much about you from my soon-to-be-former-mother-in-law. I will miss her the most. It will hurt me for years every time I think about her. They truly broke the mold when they made that one.

Maybe I have already thanked you for this, or maybe I have not! Hahahahaha, I wish I knew, but a lot of the returned notes have gone to a place where I no longer live.

Either way, I appreciate so much this beautiful tea kettle; I know that every time I am making tea (or, heck, just a Cup Noodles!) I will gratefully think of you. And then I will wonder whether you think this whole thing was just a blatant present-grab by me. Should I have returned it to you? Maybe. What would you have done with it? Returned it to Macy's, nine months later, sans gift receipt? How do I package it up?

I didn't do that because I owed some people a book three weeks ago, and I am so, so tired. I can't explain this situation to more than one person every three days, and meanwhile, your relation, whom I married, is reaching out to everyone we know to inform them that I have maybe gone crazy. I am not sure how to handle this. He is, after all, the heartbroken one, so why not give him this one last chance to center his emotional reality over mine?

Thank you so much for thinking of us!

Gratefully,
Kelly

✄

So You Want to Get into Calligraphy!

Great! Calligraphy is truly one of my very favorite crafts and one that serves me more than any other. You can practice in meetings, jazz up any mail you might want to send, pair it with other crafts, and more. It's wonderful, but it takes a lot of time to become good, and you're going to have to accept that frustration. If you're going to bail on it at the first sign of difficulty, maybe this isn't the craft for you.

Materials:

If you're just beginning, I suggest using a brush pen (see my recommendations in the supply list on page 19). I also love Tombow Dual Brush Pens. They're more marker-sized, but practicing big can be a lot easier than practicing small. If you get into it, you can go the fancy route with nibs, and ink you dip those nibs in, but that's a much more difficult, expensive, and frustrating hobby. Oh, and you'll need some paper, of course—envelopes, writing paper, what have you.

Instructions:

For the kind of calligraphy I like (read: not the heavy Gothic German kind but the swoopy, scripty stuff), there is a very simple principle: it's all about the varying thickness of the line. When you are pulling the pen down toward you, the line is thick. When the line is going away from you, it's thin. This is because of how those pen nibs I mentioned earlier work. They have two little tines as a tip, and when you're applying pressure, the two tines spread out a bit and make a thicker line.

As you will see if you try, it's much easier to put pressure on your pen on the downstroke than the upstroke. You can even do this with a ballpoint pen. Push down a little harder and move a little slower when it's coming toward you and then lighten up. (This is good advice when anything is coming toward you. Lighten up. This won't be easy.)

There are 40 bajillion YouTubes about calligraphy and some great how-to books. I'm not going to recommend a specific one, but you should get one and do the practices it suggests. I will definitely recommend *Scripts: Elegant Lettering from Design's Golden Age* by Louise Fili and Steven Heller. It's not a how-to, but it is a beautiful book that has sections on lettering from Italy, France, Germany, England, the United States, and more. It has photos of signs, hand-written letters, and full scripts and is terribly inspiring.

You can download and print guide sheets from the internet, tape them to the light tablet, put another piece of paper on top, and start practicing. Always start with a pencil. Then, just keep practicing, forever, on everything. I find that in meetings, carefully lettering the main points as I hear them is better for my memory than just try-ing to write everything down.

It can also be quite therapeutic to write out a Dark Thought as beautifully as possible, crumple it up, and throw it into a fire.

✄

So the word gets out about my impending divorce. My godpar-ents and godbrother hear about it from my soon-to-be-ex, and so do many of my friends. He talks to my sister before I do. They call me to ask if I'm okay, and I tell them I am, while internally screaming.

I only have the emotional capacity to explain it to one person every three days—and really, I'd rather just talk to the few people who already know about it—and yet my phone is exploding with concerned outreach. I know that every second that goes by when I'm sloshing around in my feelings instead of writing is a second I will regret when it's too late, and I avoid everyone.

I have made an altar in the rented room where I'm staying away from him, full of my Higher Powers council and photos of my beloved, departed Grannybarb and her sister, Aunt Corky. I am praying to it, constantly, that I can focus, do a good job on this book, do the right thing by my soon-to-be-ex, hold together, and stay sane.

On the upside, I have a Miata.

Money cannot buy happiness. But if you have $4,000, it can buy fun in the form of a 1994 Mazda Miata. This car is exceptional and perfect. It is a street-legal go-kart that someone has made into a convertible. It is the exquisite British roadster that England never managed to create. It has a goofy Fisher-Price engine—here are the spark plugs! here is where the oil goes!—that I can actually work on even though I know nothing about cars. It bounces happily up and down the RPMs and is more fun at 35 miles per hour than most cars are at 90. A Miata is more than a car—it's my *baby*—and it will live for 250,000 miles. *I love it.*

THIS IS ACTUALLY WHAT THE MIATA LOOKS LIKE. I DON'T HAVE TO DRAW A HAPPY FACE, BECAUSE IT ACTUALLY HAS ONE.

And let me tell you something: when you are driving a top-down 1994 Miata with Eleanor the Dog, you are a one-dog parade.

Eleanor is my dog and also my very heart. She's part Saint Bernard, part Muppet, and she looks like three dogs someone sewed together. She has a handsome, noble beauty that she constantly undermines with her goofiness, for she is the funniest being I have ever met. Just watching her move through the day— doing weird things with her mouth and making dinosaur noises—brings me the deepest joy.

ELEANOR

UPON-COUCH

Each morning when I wake up, she rolls over and sticks her feet in the air from happiness (this is the *only* time she rolls on her back, so I interpret it as her highest level of joy), and I say, "Good morning! Do you want to be my dog today? I think you should be my dog today! Wait, new dog, who dis?" and she makes this weird grin and runs in happy circles. At night, before I go to bed, I tell her that I'm grateful that we got another day together and she makes me happier than any dog could and then I sing the "Good Night You Can Get on the Bed No More Barking" song.

When we're sitting together in the car, our heads are the same height and color. I strap her in very carefully with a special giant-dog harness because I honestly love her more than my own life. There is nothing that delights the community more than the biggest dog in the smallest car.

But back to the Miata. I love driving and do it a lot. As a child, I dreamt of the day I could drive, and when I finally could, it was even *better* than I'd imagined. To this day, I still often feel like a 16-year-old with an infinite sense of both safety *and* freedom when my hand is on the stick. I have this small space around me that is mine, and it can be as cold or as hot as I want. Whatever music I want will be playing, at the volume I wish, and when I get sick of a song, that song will be over. In it, I can go downtown, or up to Portland, or the beach, or Mt. Hood, or Mexico, or Chile. *I can go anywhere.*

Honestly, the husband should've known something was up when I bought a '90s Miata. Things never work out for one spouse when the other has just bought a fun, impractical sports car, and what am I, if not true to form?

I drive fast through wheat fields and forest; I blast Nicki Minaj and Rich White Ladies and Beyoncé. I've made a playlist of every song I've loved since I was 15. These songs remind me that I exist and remain the same person through space and time. Sometimes, I drive to a county park when the sun finally goes down around 9:30 and watch the meteor showers by myself. For the first time since puberty, I don't wish that anyone was sitting beside me; I do not need a love interest for this to be a complete story.

I know that I can have significant and enduring relationships outside of marriage, that I can commit and rely on my closest friends as my partnerships. I know I call my own shots. Every time I look at the water tower that says INDEPENDENCE in all caps, these truths are reaffirmed.

Haha! What a dummy I am!

✂

EASY CRAFT

A Little Altar for When Things Are Good or Bad

My altar reminds me of my ancestors, other folks who I really love but aren't on the earth anymore, and pets I used to have. There are also things to remind me of the pet I *do* have, plus some things that make me appreciate my own power.

A very small BUDDHA

Materials:

You need a bunch of *anything*, any single thing in the world, as long as it brings you comfort and reminds you of the best parts of yourself. It also must fit on a surface, so smaller is better. Here is a sample list:

- Things of your beloved Grannybarb's, including a tiny stone Buddha; a little watercolor she made on the back of a Heart Care of South Louisiana appointment reminder card that says "PRACTICE"; and an airplane Bacardi bottle that she filled with water, kept in her fanny pack, and sipped from when her throat was bothering her, which is a hilarious thing to do at *any* age but especially in your late 80s.

Lil rum bottle:

The one she actually carried in her fanny pack!

RUM

MAS FINO

- Two tiny Pokémon figurines, one of which represents you because it's a teeny fox with a red head, and the other of which represents your dog, Eleanor, because it's a cute, goofy seal.

- An icon of Saint Anthony, the patron saint of lost things, who you are *constantly badgering.* You have never been Catholic, and only part of your family is culturally Catholic, and yet Saint Anthony is your favorite uncle. At least four times per week you're hitting him up for something: "Saint Anthony, Saint Anthony, won't you look around? Something's been lost and it needs to be found." You do this for small items but also when something bigger is lost—you ask him to find a way for you, or for someone else. You ask if he can find you some serenity to just accept whatever bullshit is happening.

- A small icon for the patron saint of animals, Saint Francis of Assisi, because you love Saint Francis and also you really want him to keep an eye on Eleanor.

- A picture of your Grannybarb and her sisters when they were teenagers (they were all so hot, it's kinda stupid) plus your great-grandmother, who is laughing, and your great-grandfather, who looks super pleased to be sitting on a couch with his happy wife and smoke-show daughters.

- A little-bitty picture of the pope because you are so fond of him and the Jesuits.

Appointment-reminder-
-card cum Zen instruction.

44

- A framed picture of Lakshmi that a Hindu friend gave you in 2011 to bring you love and happiness. This has *absolutely* happened, and so now you have this very beautiful small picture of Her, draped in sparkly jewelry and pearls, and have scattered some loose cut gems in front (that She would like).

- Some of those Mexican dioramas of clay skeletons wearing cute clothes and just going about their business, except all the walls are covered in glitter. This is a nice reminder that it's possible to have fun when you and your friends are dead.

- Teeny felt balls in various sea colors.

- The Empress and Queen of Cups Tarot cards. I could explain them, but whatever. You can go read the descriptions of those cards if you're *that* interested.

- Things move on and off the altar, and that's okay! When they are not in active display/use, they live in a little IKEA tub that says "ALTAR" in gold sparkly washi tape on the top.

Instructions:

1. **First, figure out a good location for your altar.** I would *not* suggest the floor, especially if you have pets, but it's nice to set it in a place where you can sit down and gaze upon it. I have mine above this little cabinet I got at HomeGoods.

2. **Think about whether you want to put down some sort of cloth.** Good options could be a pretty scarf or a fat quarter of fabric in a pattern you like from JOANN. (Don't forget to look for a coupon first, because the store constantly offers 50-percent-off-one-item coupons.)

3. **Think about what Higher Powers you want represented on there.** I have a council of Higher Powers that I appeal to, one that includes everyone from God to former Texas governor Ann Richards but also has deities of several different religions, aforementioned ancestors, and the spirits of childhood pets. It's basically everyone on the ethereal plane I feel would have my best interests at heart.

4. **Things that represent said Higher Power(s) get the prime real estate.** I think about creating clusters around who would like one another, so all my saints and God stuff are in one area, but so is Buddha. There's also an ancestor area, plus a framed picture of Ann Richards when I can fit it, which I currently cannot, but I feel like she is a very practical woman and would understand. Noting that this is sacrilegious is a valid critique, but it is my altar, and you can make yours however you see fit.

5. **Get the things that remind you of the best parts of you.** This could be the qualities your mother loves in you or the things you have done or are capable of doing, even if maybe not right now. Something that represents you at your kindest and/or strongest. This can be anything. It can be a penny that you hold while you remember these things about yourself. Just get that Best You on there.

6. **Add things that delight you, if there is room.** Those dumb little felt balls are just *so cute*, they remind me of tiny sprites/things in a Miyazaki movie/candy. On they go!

7. **Look at all of it.** Maybe silently ask your Higher Power(s) if they're down with how things are looking. If it doesn't feel right, go ahead and move it! You can even move it off the altar altogether if you need to, without hurting any spiritual feelings. The whole thing has to feel cohesive and right.

8. **When it's done, hang out by it!** Make it a regular thing! I can't say that I am next to my altar all the time, or even every day, but I like to have this place in my house to go. I try to say thank you a bunch, especially when I am super sad or afraid about everything. But I also just go and talk to it. "Hey, I'm really super afraid of XYZ," or "I feel like shit about my life," or "I just have no fucking idea what to do right now," and then I'm quiet for a bit. Obviously, it's not like a voice just pops into my head telling me what to do (although, actually, every now and again that *does* happen and it's exceptionally convenient), but it feels lazy not to at least ask.

Tips for arranging: Put larger things in the back and smaller things up front. Remember that the eye needs places to rest, so some empty space is great, *but* it's better to get everyone and everything on there that needs to be. Things look better in odd-numbered groups. I don't know why. They just do.

✂

When I flee my marriage, I rent, via Airbnb, a beautiful room full of plants in a giant Craftsman owned by Camille, the world's most lovely hospice nurse (as opposed to all those selfish fuckers you normally find tending to the dying).

Camille, once upon a time, also fled an unhappy marriage. She feels certain that I will be okay, and as she is someone who sees so many *not* okay people, I choose to have faith in this. When I tell people that I am getting unmarried (it feels better to say than "divorced"), from those who have gone through it, I get one of two responses.

Many (but not all) men who have gotten divorced look stricken; they take on a thousand-yard stare and then grasp my forearm or pull me in for a hug.

"I'm so sorry," they say, eyes downcast. A lip is bitten; a deep sigh is sighed. "Divorce is hell."

Then they tell their stories, which are so horrifying and disorienting. They thought they lived in ancient sea forts that would endure forever but were actually residing in sandcastles with itty-bitty toothpick flags. Now, they are not sure anything is real. I do not and cannot know what is real, they tell me, for this is the natural outcome of divorce, but take heart: in five or ten years, God willing, I *might* be back to normal.

With this group, I try to effect a solemn expression. I know it would be inappropriate to express glee.

That glee, I'd find, is shared by most (but not all) of the women who have gotten divorces . . . and quite a few who haven't.

"Good for you," one says quietly, looking around to see who might hear, even though we're alone in her beautiful living room. "I had to wait *ages* for Harold to die."

"Oh, you did the *right thing*," says another. "I left my first husband, and two years later, I found the most perfect man in the world. We've never argued since."

"You're so lucky that you can. I couldn't have, not then; I didn't have any way to support myself or the kids," say the 70- and 80-somethings, and I pause to marvel that I am allowed to work and own property, that I do not have kids with him, that I can cut ties and *go*.

I still owe some people a book and am desperately trying to write it, mostly on a wrought-iron table in Hospice Nurse Camille's garden. I wander over to Jimmy Z's gas station and shoot the shit with the locals and smoke a bunch of cigarettes. I go to the new, hip bar in a converted gas station, even though I am not drinking, although I am also not attending meetings. I arrange and rearrange the altar I have made on my desk. It does indeed bring me temporary peace, although inevitably all the dread sloshes back in without warning. Then I go pray there again, thinking that perhaps I will square the circle of this book, figure out how not to upset anyone while doing the least-acceptable thing.

I also have the Mechanic to smooch.

I've had a life-threatening crush on him for a couple years. His shop was exquisitely clean, and in his office, he had multiple bookshelves full of everything. He had the lowest voice, he was

6-feet-14, and his shoulders were 7 miles across. He was like an *extremely* hot refrigerator that I *really* wanted to fuck. His hands were the size of the moon. His face was more beautiful than the moon. *He is teaching me how to race my car, and he has grease on his hands.* Of *course* I started carrying on with him. It would have been criminally negligent to do otherwise.

For a variety of reasons, it was not meant to be, but for the recently unmarried, *I cannot recommend carrying on with your mechanic/racing instructor highly enough.*

I am so, so excited for my future. I realize that, despite what everyone has told me and I have deeply internalized, I don't have to have a husband to qualify as a human. If I want kids, I can have them *without* being in a shitty relationship. Life is open and available and full of possibilities.

Let's fast-forward a couple months and see how that's going.

CHAPTER 2

Ascendant

In Which I Establish a New Family,
Join Tinder, and Fall in Love
over the Course of One Evening

EVERYTHING WAS UNSETTLING THAT SUMMER IN A WAY that has nothing to do with my little domestic drama playing out in a small Oregon town.

Fifty people are gunned down in a gay dance club in Orlando. There is an attempted coup in Turkey against the nationalist prime minister; it is quickly and violently crushed. The Black Lives Matter movement is threatened when a lone wolf shoots a bunch of police officers in Dallas.

There is a horrible new voice and face everywhere, because summer 2016 is also the summer of the worst American.

Soon, I tell myself, he will be defeated by an incredibly qualified woman. I don't love this woman, but I respect her, and this is more than enough.

When I was seven, I saw his hideous face on the cover of a tabloid at Eckerd's Pharmacy—he was probably getting divorced, or talking shit, or just being his entirely unbearable self—and asked my father who he was.

"Donald Trump is a bad man, with more money than taste," he replied.

This seemed fair and served me well as a guiding principle; I needed nothing of what he offered and had carefully avoided him ever since. Now, I had to dedicate so much mental space to him and his face that looks like the behind of a chicken with a pursed little asshole mouth. I assumed that after the election, he'd fuck off to whatever second-rate news channel he'd planned on starting, and I could go back to pretending he doesn't exist.

Things for me personally, however, are a bit more settled. I've rented a little house in my old Salem neighborhood, handed in the book, and figured out the dog custody arrangements. (We didn't do split custody—too white even for me.)

My social circle has shrunk dramatically—most of my friends are up in Portland, 50 miles north—but two of my very best friends, Carrie and Emily, live down here, and the three of us are together constantly. The fourth member of this group, Margaret, lives in Portland but it's only a 45-minute drive, so we see her all the time.

Margaret was actually my introduction to the group. We became friends when she messaged me on Facebook in 2010. She knew of me from my column and music coverage in the local paper. She was in the Canary Islands, doing something adventurous, and was like, "Hey—you're funny and smart. We should be friends." Ten months later she was back in town, and one day I walked by her while she was smoking outside a bar.

"Hey! Aren't you Kelly Williams Brown?" she said, and so I sat down to have a cigarette and asked her what she was up to.

"As soon as I'm done here, I'm getting into an elf costume and heading over to the history museum," she said, and I was smitten, consumed with a desire to myself be an elf at Willamette Heritage Center's Christmas extravaganza. I could not hold this inside me and expressed this new but overwhelming wish.

"Oh, for sure," she said. "Hopefully this year? Or if not, definitely next year. What day works for you?"

A month later, I met Carrie and Emily at Margaret's birthday party, but I truly got to know them two weeks later when the three of us headed up to visit Margaret at the hippie resort where she was cooking—an expensive, clothing-optional hot springs that boasted vegetarian food, yoga, and the *very* fun staff-only cabins, where we got to stay.

I brought the Ungame, which is my favorite. It's a noncompetitive, nonthreatening game developed by 1970s therapists, and it makes people so uncomfortable, unless they sense true board game genius when they encounter it. There is no winning and no end to the game, which is why the box suggests building a consensus around a time limit. You can go either direction on the board, which is speckled with places like "Complaint Campground" and "Compliment Cove." You draw cards that are labeled "Light Hearted" or "Deeper Understanding,"  although they are all uncomfortably personal and/or weird. Think, "What is something about your father you would change?" or "Say something about earthquakes." Everyone loved it.

We drank whiskey and hung out in the staff-only hot spring,

and then naked in the sauna, and laughed about the sweet dingus who tried, unsuccessfully, to seduce us one by one. We talked about how no man has ever invited a woman over to his house to listen to a record, even if that's the stated purpose, and then we made crafts and stayed up all night laughing.

That was six years prior, and they'd been my primary friend group ever since.

The summer I left my husband, there was a lot of sitting around backyard fires, a lot of Tarot, a lot of yelling about sexuality and power and the systems that entangle us, and also a lot of Emily playing silly original compositions on her ukulele.

Carrie is sort of the leader of the group, although she'd laugh in your face if you said that. There's a strong Cool Lesbian vibe to her, and everyone seeks her approval. She's the kind of person who was the lead singer in multiple bands and also traveled through India by herself at 19 and, one winter, decided to take the train to North Dakota and work as a cook in the oil fields.

One time I was really excited for her birthday party because I'd made her some stickers to put on bar bathroom mirrors that said "EVERY MOMENT YOU SPEND CRITICIZING YOUR APPEARANCE IS A MOMENT YOU AREN'T SMASHING THE PATRIARCHY," but then literally *everyone* there had made her a very special present, including multiple original musical creations and a diorama of her and her dog together on their favorite mountain.

Carrie was fiercely loyal to the people she deemed smart enough to be worth her time, but she had very little patience for people she saw as either too pretentious or not sharp enough to keep up. "People see me as mean. I'm not mean," she once said. "I'm just bored by most people."

Emily is like a decadent courtier who traveled forward in time and manifested as an extremely chill Oregon girl with hair like a dandelion. She is both very regal and very silly. She's also the most supportive and kind friend I have ever had—multiple people, including me, want Emily to marry them just so she could be their wife and have, as she puts it, her "friendly cloud energy" forever. She has the best laugh, and she laughs at everything.

She was a dandelion in more than one way, floating from place to place implacably, in a car that seemed held together with duct tape. Money was not of interest to her. What was of interest was being as loving and loyal as possible to her friends. In this arena, she had great success.

We would go to the local pub in the evenings and smoke cigarettes around the large outdoor fire pit and drink giant $4 mugs of dry cider. Carrie would rant about dwindling wolf populations, or neoliberal responses to houselessness, or food insecurity, and discuss her love for the socialist grandpas she mixed with during their socialist-grandpas-and-Carrie meetings.

I've also made a new friend, Brooke, which is big news since I only ever want to have, like, five friends at once. Brooke is exactly 10 years younger than me, she has the same job at the same newspaper I had when I was her age, and we get along like a house on fire. Brooke is hysterically funny, and we have very similar brains. We don't have to explain our absurd actions or feelings because the other would've done and felt the same thing.

So: friends are in order. House is in order, with a little yard for Eleanor to sprint around in and protect us from squirrels, which, as far as she is concerned, are the greatest possible threat to our liberty and way of life. I have a little break, professionally, while I wait to do edits on the book. Things are settled and divided with soon-to-be-former-husband. And now comes the moment I have been waiting for: Tinder!

I'd been so, so excited to use that dumb app. I don't think there even were any dating apps last time I was single. I've always wanted some sort of *Bachelorette*-style situation where I could assemble a bunch of men in the room to judge them. This was somewhat like that, *and I could do it from the tub!*

Plus, not that I would've ever broken up with someone to get to Tinder, but I was pretty bummed on having missed out on it. I'd gotten to use the app on behalf of my single friends, which was a blast. I knew it wouldn't be good, but I resented never getting to experience the chaos of the thing.

And then it was really, really fun. Unpopular opinion, but: all I dreamed and more.

Like everyone recently out of a relationship, part of me was convinced that I was now singularly disqualified from love and would never have a relationship again. After all, I was a 31-year-old crone wandering through the world, my very footsteps turning fertile soil to ash. My uterus, I assumed, had dried up like a tum-

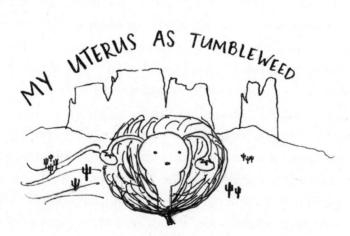

bleweed and blown away; surely it was rolling through Montana by now.

But maybe, just maybe, I could find some equally pathetic man who would take pity on me and grow to love me despite all this.

Then I got on Tinder, and it was like that GIF of a woman having 16 hot dogs thrown at her face. Turns out there were *plenty* of men who were down to chat with an ancient 31-year-old. I now have four years' experience, on-and-off, with Tinder. I have found some incredible people, some relationships, some new prestige TV, and just the right amount of disillusionment.

Things I have learned from men on Tinder:

1. *Succession* is an excellent show that I should watch.

2. It's okay to sleep with someone you like and care about even if it won't end in a relationship. It's funny how this took me 32 years to absorb.

3. Most guys shouldn't be slept with.

There are extremely interesting (and good and bad and worthwhile and unworthy) people on Tinder, just like there are extremely interesting (and good and bad and worthwhile and un-worthy) people everywhere. I went out with a diplomat, an inven-tor, a composer, a nuclear physicist, a British YouTuber, and, in an especially delightful dalliance, a legit rocket scientist for NASA who my friends called Space Daddy. These were and are lovely men I definitely would not have met otherwise.

More things the generous gents on Tinder have taught me include:

4. JUULing is better (read: healthier, subtler, and more convenient) than smoking but also a million times more embarrassing.

5. *Chapo Trap House.*

6. You should not, on the first date, ask someone if they're seeing other people. Turns out that makes your date very uncomfortable! I had no idea.

7. If you meet someone, go on a few dates, really enjoy them but find the connection isn't there for one or both of you, that's actually great. It's the one circumstance I've found where I can be friends with a straight guy. You three know who you are.

8. Fuckboys can seem so sincere! It took me a couple encounters to realize their game. The reason they're not texting is not because they like me *too* much.

9. There is no excuse for someone in his mid-30s to be a bad kisser. Has no one told you that your tongue is too active and assertive, sir? I mean, I didn't tell you, but *someone* should!

In the course of my Tinder fall, I met a lot of guys, heard a lot of stories, smooched some, figured out how to extricate myself after one drink, developed lines to cleverly explain away my brief marriage, and remembered that I truly like men, despite some obvious flaws. It's a trip, especially when you're dating in a (relatively) small dating pool, like the one in my part of Oregon. For example, I eventually realized—because various dates mentioned her, as she does similar work to me—that there is a woman who has dated three of the men I have dated and gone on dates with countless more. I want so, so badly to reach out to her to get to the bottom of this. And become best friends? Fight to the death for the hand of Portland's fourth most eligible software engineer? It's fun to think about.

It came down to this: Tinder isn't great, but it beats not trying. I'm grateful for the chance to get to meet someone new, to ask about their life, and to find out about things I'd never otherwise know.

There's the dark side, of course. Tinder tells us there is an endless supply of humans, which is a corrosive and dangerous assumption to hold. You can forget that this random person is, indeed, a person. And although you shouldn't imagine your future together, you also shouldn't dislike them before you've met them. It only takes one, and there truly is a lid for every pot.

Oh, and one more piece of hard-won Tinder dating advice: do not, under any circumstances, go out with someone who has written "Good vibes only!" on his profile, because that doesn't mean, "I'm a generally sunny person who works hard on happiness and tries to go with the flow." It means, "I will act like you're having your period *at* me."

By the early fall, I'd gone on a few dates but nothing interesting.

Well, okay, that's not true. I went on some extremely interesting dates with a Frenchman named Henri (*ahhhhhn-REE!* So infinitely better than dumb anglophone *Henry*).

On our first date, he sat down across from me in the booth, scooched over, and clamped his knees together around mine, forcing my kneecaps together uncomfortably. He kept my legs in this surprising, not-at-all comfortable grip for the next 15 minutes. I didn't know how to address it because I had never even considered that this was something that could happen. This will be a running theme for the next two years of my life.

He leaned forward. "You ah very, uhhh, zexeee?" he says, "although—I wheeel tell you now?—I do not like redheads, very much."

I wait for him to finish this sentence, but he is done. I couldn't tell if Henri was a sociopath or his was just the French way. I didn't want to be culturally insensitive, so I kept saying yes to dates.

At some point, I go over to his apartment to hang out, although I've specified ahead of time that I will absolutely not be sleeping with him.

We're making out, I stop to adjust my dress, and then, when I turn back, he has stood up and whipped out his—and I'm not trying to be unkind here, this is just the truth—not-great dick, which is now within a foot of my face. I sort of goggle at it. I'd given no indication that I'd like his dick to be here, right now, and yet it is.

"What the *fuck*, dude?" I ask, and he looks bewildered, so very, very confused as to what I could possibly be reacting to right now.

"There eeze a problem?" he asks, brow furrowed.

"Yeah, Henri! Yeah, there *is* a problem. Okay . . . I'm, um, I'm going to . . . leave," I say as I stand up.

He looks shocked—shocked!—by this turn of events.

"You ahhh leaving? Right *now*?"

"Yes! Yes, Henri, I am *definitely leaving*."

He sighs and gazes off into space. Without looking back at me, he says—so wistfully!—"You were an ahstehhhh-ROID."

This is so damn good that I can't handle it, and almost start laughing but decide that this is a Serious Moment.

"Yeah. Yeah, I *am*," I say. I didn't realize until that moment that I had always needed a man to acknowledge and sadly remark upon my asteroidness as I stomped out of his life *forever*. Tinder made that dream come true!

For maybe the first time ever, I was fine—dang, delighted!—to not be in a relationship. If I wanted to, I could go on four dates per week, but I didn't particularly *feel* like it. I was feeling so, so independent, so happy to live in my own space where nobody was ever yelling at me. I never wanted a man in my house again, even though I adore them, because I was so, so happy with just Eleanor the Dog and me.

My plans for the future starred not a man but my friends. The grand plan was to get a bunch of land and form a big compound among us, support one another, help raise kids, and work on a garden. If I had a man in my life and he was into it, he could live in his own structure and fix our cars and handle, like, sinks clogged with hair, and in exchange, date and fuck whomever he wanted.

Then, one day, I'd matched with someone I will call Shockingly Attractive Man, and the trajectory of my life turned.

Sam, as I will call him (get it?!), was—is—beautiful. He looks like Jon Hamm but sometimes makes Paul Rudd faces, and this is exactly as devastating as you'd imagine. He's one of those people who are so hot that you sort of stumble on your words around them.

But I don't notice this at first. When I first lay eyes on him, I feel the deepest relief. *Oh. Here you are. I didn't know I'd been waiting.*

There's a Japanese phrase, "*koi no yokan.*" It's not love at first sight but rather the premonition of love—the sense, upon meeting someone, that you will love them.

I've had this several times in my life. It happened when I met my friend Marissa the first day of nerd camp. Even as a 13-year-old, she was so beautiful and so cool, the kind of person I figured would never give my nerdy self the time of day. And yet, I made a joke and she threw her head back and laughed uproariously. She would go on to pretty much singlehandedly explain hair, makeup, fashion, and boys to me.

There was the time, during my Hurricane Katrina semester of college, when I was a reporter for the student newspaper and needed a quote about something-or-other from someone in student government. I went down to the office, and there was this tall, lanky man with dark, shaggy hair in a UCLA hoodie.

"Hi, I'm Kelly, the higher-ed reporter for the *Daily Emerald*, and I need a quote about such-and-such," I began.

He started to talk and seemed remarkably well-informed, and he was so goddamn cute that I kept gazing at his beatific face rather than writing down what he was saying. The more he talked, the more entranced I became. I realized he'd never told me his name or position. Trying to be sneaky, as though I knew his name but needed to be super-super accurate, I said, "Umm, could I have you spell your first name for me?"

He looked confused. "Uh, sure, it's A-D-A-M."

"And your last?"

"Uhh, M-I-L-L-E-R."

"Yes, yes, of course. Okay, um, and your title?"

"I'm . . . student body president?" He said it slowly, in a concerned tone, as if he was worried I might have suffered from a stroke while interviewing him.

He squinted at me. "Didn't we have speech class together freshman year?"

And then this enormous smile spread across his face—just gorgeous, with perfect white teeth and crinkled brown eyes. My eyes widened, I froze, and something rushed up within me, like a spring out of the earth—*You will be mine, you will, you will love me, you will fall asleep next to me every night, I will know every inch of your body*—and then time started again and I said, "Uhh, yeah, I think maybe we did? Haha, funny!"

Sixteen months later, he would pack all his items into his green Volvo with wood paneling, drive down to Mississippi, and move into my little carriage house with me, because, as far as I was concerned, I had foretold this, willed it into being slowly over months and months. That was our fourth date, and of course it didn't work, but that's a story for another time.

Because this is what I do. Every three or four years, I see a man and I *know*, and then I will wait until time and circumstances are right—sometimes years, with lesser relationships in between. I write the entire story before I've met the main character, and I don't leave room for edits.

Anyway, all those experiences came close to the fabled *koi no yokan* sensation, but I'd never, ever felt it like I did with Shockingly Attractive Man. It was this insane feeling of relief: *Oh, here you are! Finally!*

I didn't actually fall over (which I have done when overwhelmed with feeling), but I do remember sort of collapsing onto the diner chair.

I sit down across from Sam, look at his face, and I register that he's super fucking hot, so that's great, too.

We'd matched earlier that day on Tinder. I messaged him and asked what he was up to. He wasn't up to anything. Should we meet at the truck stop that is precisely halfway between Salem and Portland? The one with a Popeyes? He makes a pro-Popeyes comment; I am undone. We should meet, yes, let's do that in a couple hours.

Side note: Popeyes Exceptionalism is a hill I will happily die upon Monday, Tuesday, Wednesday, Thursday, Friday, and weekends by appointment. As J. Kenji López-Alt said, "[In] every city that has a Popeyes, Popeyes serves the best fried chicken in that city." He's sort of kidding, but mostly not. No matter how dark life is, it will always be 25 percent better when I am just about to eat some Popeyes. This love is foundational.

As we explore the truck stop—the arcade, the showers, the convenience store with an entire trucking accessory and clothing section—we try to one-up each other about our Popeyes love.

"I don't think you understand," I told him. "I used to drive an hour and fifteen minutes to get to the one up in Portland."

"I don't think *you* understand," he replied. "My last serious girlfriend was a vegan, and I mostly gave up meat, but I couldn't give up Popeyes, which is, like, the most offensive meat you can have. I'd always carefully eat it outside, watching out for crumbs, cleaning up any as I went, and then I'd sneak out the remains to the garbage can and cover it with other garbage so it wouldn't offend her."

I was dazzled that he was 1) so dedicated to Popeyes but 2) thoughtful enough to try to shield her from it, and 3) impressed, if slightly alarmed, that he was able to date a vegan for three years. Sorry, vegans! You're making the only valid moral choice, and we all know it, but life without cured hams and expensive cheeses feels like life without sex. Sure, you could do it, but what's the point?

Neither of us is ready to call it a night, because—although I don't know it yet—both of us are victim to classic addict thinking: if three is good, then nine is *three* times as good.

Should we go to the small town that was five miles away through the country? We should. Oh, wow, we were both divorced. It's rough but also the best decision we ever made. Yes, I am still technically married, and I understand if that bothers him, but it does not.

The bar here is mediocre. In fact, I do not like this small town as much as I like the Bavarian-themed one another few miles down the road. Should we go there? I'm not drinking, so I can drive us in the Miata, which barely has space for one person. I can drive us wherever. I could drive us to Mexico.

He tells me, later, that in the teeny passenger seat he felt the gravity. That he'd been in a before, and he was now moving to an after. "I don't know what this is, but it's going to be *something*," was how he later describes it.

If it's not all-consuming, I'm not interested (*healthyhealthy-healthysohealthy!*). I don't want to see you tonight and then again in four days with intermittent texting; *I want to go to bed for four days*. I want to call in sick to work. I don't want you to like me; I want you to feel like you can't believe I exist and now you can't live without me. This, for me, is *the* high, way better than any drink or drug or yoga or eating or not eating or cigarettes or any of the things I do to feel slightly different than the baseline for a few minutes.

I'm so familiar with—or perhaps always listening for—the clack-clack-clacking of the roller coaster being dragged up the incline. Maybe that just sounds like a successful date to me. Anyway, Sam is looking at me, and I'm close enough to smell him, and *~*~clacking intensifies~*~*.

We arrive in my favorite small town and head into a bar. I order a Diet Coke, and he orders whatever. It is the Saturday before Halloween and the bars are full, but none of this registers with me. Every little receptor in my brain is overwhelmed by these very happy chemicals because *here he is.* I feel sparkly, powerful, magical, as if I have called him into being.

I have this theory that the kernel of every relationship's demise can and will be vocalized on the first date. In this case, we discuss how dark our lives have been, at times, and then contrast it with who we are now. We don't know it, but we are listing the things that will be stripped from us, that we will strip from each other, while we are together.

He tells me that, over the last few years, he has found a quiet calm within himself. He has accepted a lot about himself, and that grace makes it much easier to exist in the world. "Wow," I say, "you know, I've really done that, too. It is what I'm most proud of, in fact."

We talk about our unhappy marriages. We talk about how we have both been people who will historically stick with something long, long after it is dead. We talk about how we have found the strength to be on our own. We laugh with delight about how hard this work has been and how glad we are to have done it. We talk about how we will never again stay in a bad relationship as it decays because we are afraid to be alone.

It's fun to smugly discuss something you think is the trunk of yourself but is actually just a plastic bag on a spindly branch.

I sense, in ways that I still cannot articulate and surely wasn't experiencing consciously, that his pain is like mine, that we have similar scars. He is so, so bright, and quiet-funny, which is my favorite kind of funny, and he laughs at all my jokes. He has worked in politics; he once built a food cart, including a six-foot wood-fired pizza oven from scratch; he shows me pictures of his enormous organic garden full of fruits and vegetables; he is so well-read; and, it is hard to overemphasize this, he looks like Jon Hamm.

At some point, I say something and his eyes flash dark, and for a moment, I see his face fleetingly crumple before the mask comes back on. And let me tell you, dear reader, that there is nothing I love more than a moody man, and there is nothing *any* of us love more than someone who pushes our fucked-up childhood buttons.

We get back in my car to drive back to the truck stop, and he asks if he can kiss me, and yes, duh. So then we make out in the Miata for a good 15 minutes and this, too, is magical.

So of course, since spending some time with this guy is good, spending every moment with him will be even better. I ask him if he wants to come down to Salem the next night. I will make him gumbo. I will cook this astonishing and complicated soup that requires me to stand next to the stove, stirring, for at least 45 minutes. I will do this in a black slip. This is my wildcard, and I'm playing it early, but who caaaaaares—I AM IN LOVE!

He does want this. He comes down the next night, I cook for him, and then we mess around as a tremendous windstorm rolls in from the west. It howls over the eaves of my bedroom, and as we stay up all night, I tell him there is a 66.7 percent chance we're going to fall in love. He laughs, and I ask him if I'm wrong, and he agrees that I am not wrong, and then we roll around some more.

Boundaries! Someday I will (please, God) have them, but October 30, 2016, was not that day.

After he leaves, I immediately text Brooke—"Update: I just met my next husband." Carrie, Emily, and I get together that night at the little pub we always go to. It's literally a public house—the owner's ex-wife's house, actually—and it has all sorts of little-bitty rooms, and nooks and crannies, and a big fire pit outside where everyone sits together and chats. There are 25-year-olds and 85-year-olds, and there's no hard liquor, only beer, wine, and cider, which means no one ever gets too drunk. The bartenders have been there for 10 years, and they always know what I want.

That night, we put our feet up to the fire, sit our drinks on the brick ledge, and I tell them everything—every single exchange, every beat and pat and silence. Despite the fact that everyone's listened to me talk about my divorce for months, they are genuinely happy for me.

Perler Bead Trivets Are Forever

This is a good craft for those who are six years old and/or don't have one or both of their arms, which I soon won't. It also *really* impresses guys when you make them one.*

Materials:

- Perler beads
- A Perler bead mat
  (It's clear and has tiny spikes you will carefully set each individual bead onto.)
- An iron
- Parchment paper

IT'S GONNA LOOK LIKE ONE OF THESE:

Instructions:

1. You can determine a pattern ahead of time, I guess? Probably good to have a vague idea of what you eventually want this trivet to look like. I certainly never grid it out, but I don't know the level of planning you like to see in your life. If you want to do that, do that. I usually just make weird geometric patterns. I tend to like the hexagonal geometry patterns above the square ones, but again, this is *your* trivet and should have the angles *you* like.

---

* Sorta? They'll be nice about it, at least.

2. Set the beads upright on the teeny spikes, times 250 or whatever, according to the pattern in your head or on the paper. Be
careful not to bump it with your hand because those dumb
little tubes *will* tip over and roll chaotically for no reason at all.
Perler beads: they're just like us!

3. When you have the trivet of your dreams and you're ready to
make it forever, heat your iron to medium.

4. Place parchment paper on top of your design. Slowly move the
iron in a circular motion over the parchment-paper-covered
beads. Make sure you're constantly moving the iron. Look, it
doesn't matter what you're doing: *any time* you're using an
iron, you should be constantly moving it. This craft is no exception.

5. Wait 30 seconds or so and then carefully peel back the parchment paper. See how melted the beads look. They should look
really melted.

6. When the trivet is cool, carefully
peel it off the mat. Examine it
for structural integrity, perhaps even flexing it lightly
this way and that. Hon-
estly, the top third of the
beads, and ideally more,
should be melted through.
You probably didn't do it
enough the first time. Do
it again.

PERLER BEADS:
- VERY SMALL.
- VERY CHAOTIC.

7. Give it to Sam. He will put it on the little half-bookshelf in his hallway. Even when things get terribly bad with him—and they will, sooner than you'd imagine—you can spot this and the other crafts you've made him around his house and think, *Well, okay, he loves me enough that he wants to look at this, at least.*

CHAPTER 3

Dislocated

In Which Trump Becomes President, My Bones Crumble to Dust, and We All Become 25 to 33 Percent Crazier

THERE'S SOME OTHER BIG STUFF GOING ON AS I'M FALLING head over heels for this new guy and being an awful recently-in-love person.

Here, there, everywhere, every day, in almost every conversation: the only topic on everyone's lips is the 2016 presidential election. To be honest, I'm having a very hard time thinking about anything else, even as I'm being swept away by this tide. I listen to every political podcast. I leave MSNBC on in the background as I'm doing the dishes. I reflexively visit election-statistics website FiveThirtyEight when I start to feel panicky, which I do *all the time*. (*Hillary is going to win! Nate Silver says so!*) I think that maybe if I read every bit of *POLITICO* and breathe deeply, I won't feel this sickness.

Sam says he can't talk about the election anymore. I don't need to press him on his thoughts because I know they are just like mine. Just one more bit of evidence that we are meant to be.

Another exhibit: as nervous as we both are about the election itself, we both *love* Election Day. We've been talking, so much, about policy; about his experiences working in the legislature; about our nearly identical political beliefs; and, above all, how much we care about this process—the fact that everyone gets together and chooses who we want to be, that everyone gets the same vote. I always cry as I'm waiting in line to drop off my ballot—it just makes me so happy. Democracy, yaaaaay!!!!

We spend Election Day together, driving around in the country to a joyful iTunes mix I made. Before I see him, I drop my divorce paperwork in the mail because, again and always, I conduct myself like the protagonist of a second-tier Nora Ephron novel. Just imagine, leaving my bad marriage on the same day we get our first female president!

So of course there will be much to celebrate. He and I will be together at the big Democratic Party of Oregon gathering in the convention center. I will wear a 1960s powder-blue dress suit with pearls, and he will be in a smart navy suit with a tasteful tie, and we will look phenomenal. Tonight's the night he meets all my friends, and I am so excited to introduce them to the man I now assume will be my next husband, because I am a lunatic.

We grab drinks beforehand to watch the election coverage. I'm watching the bar TVs in confusion. I start to see something alarming. He has won Ohio. He looks good in Michigan. Although the many TVs are tuned to different channels, they are all telling me the same thing: what I'd never allowed myself to imagine now seems to be coming to pass.

A weirdly biological panic rises in me. I must find safety. For the first and only time I can recall, I have a hysterical tiny mammal feeling—*find a hollow. Shelter in place. Stay there until this is no longer happening.*

I literally want to crawl under the keno machine, and I am disappointed when I bend over and see they are flush with the floor. What about the video poker machine, could I fit there? I would like to fold up my arms and legs and be a little tiny ball, face pressed against the disgusting bar carpet, which feels safer than sitting here in this moment. Anything is safer than this.

I breathe deeply and tell myself that the floor won't actually help. With every moment that passes, I, Sam, my friends, and horrified strangers are hurtling together into this absolutely batshit reality. Surely it's a joke. It's *not* a joke, but nor could it *possibly* be real.

We leave the bar and head to the convention center. Hundreds of people are sitting on the floor, so I guess I wasn't the only one who received the get-on-the-ground memo. Many are crying. I'm not crying because, you see, it's not real.

We can't stay here. What do I want to do? I want to see my mom. We drive out to her house, about 12 minutes away, me and this man I am sure I will be in love with but have known for only 10 days. He, quite understandably, is drunk. Whatever, I'm not going to make it through this administration sober. My sobriety is going to last about another week.

My mother, out of everyone in the world, is the best at making me feel better. She gives me very tough-love pep talks that end with her conviction that I can handle whatever it is and will be okay. She gives the best advice and is, almost certainly, the reason I am a successful advice-giver. I got it from my mamma!

I want her to do that tonight, but how could she possibly?

"What's going to happen?" I ask her, even though when it comes to politics I'm the obsessive one. I want her to tell me that it'll be okay, that what I think is happening is not what is actually happening.

"I don't know. I don't know," she says, shaking her head. "I don't know."

Of course she doesn't. No one knows what is going to happen, and we sit out on her back porch in silence. My mother offers Sam some nice bourbon, which he sucks down. She has now met the man I've been dating for all of nine days, and that was the least-weird thing that happened that night.

We all just sit there, stunned, and I smoke cigarette after cigarette and pray that what seems to be happening is not, that this is a dream, that there has been a terrible mistake, that this is not the world we're all living in together.

You know those two bodies in Pompeii who died in each other's arms? That was Sam and me for a week after the election, just lying together in bed clinging to each other and waiting for the ash to cover us. Honestly, we had been spending a lot of time in bed anyway, but the tenor changed, and we truly leaned in to our bewilderment, misery, and terror. He worked from home, and I didn't really work at all, so we were free to lie around waiting for the end of the world, punctuated by thousand-yard-stare sex.

I'm a well-off woman in a blue state and didn't have anything personally consequential to lose with his election, aside from a foundationally sunny view of democracy, plus I guess a sense of stability knowing he was not the human in charge of the world's largest arsenal of nuclear weapons. My horror at this miscarriage was strictly intellectual, and I know it was infinitely worse for many, many people.

But it punctured and broke things within me that I didn't know were there to be punctured and broken. If you are reading this, and you do not like him, you know what that night was like. You know what the subsequent nights (weeks, months, years) have been like. And maybe you, too, haven't felt entitled to your own fear, because you—unlike those people in concentration camps— are in no immediate danger.

For me, it cracked a core belief, one that helps me live peace- fully in the world, and made my main spiritual practice nearly impossible.

It's a slightly modified Buddhist meditation I do, and I highly recommend it. First, I think of Eleanor and my Grannybarb, two beings for whom I feel nothing but the purest love, the wake-up- and-thank-God-every-morning gratitude.

I hold that feeling in my heart for a moment, to get it nice and settled in, and then I try to transfer it to myself and say, "May I be well, happy, and peaceful." I extend it to people in my life who have brought me to a new place, introduced a new way of think- ing, or just remind me of who I am working to become, saying, "May my teachers be well, happy, and peaceful." I do and say the same thing for my family and then my friends, all while trying to extend that same deep, uncritical love to each and every one.

Then it's the indifferent people: the sweet people at my local 7-Eleven or any random person I may have seen that day. I also wish for them to be well, happy, and peaceful.

Now, here is the very hard part: I try, *so hard*, to extend that same love and hope for goodness to the unfriendly person, and in this case, I try to think of the people I feel the very least friendly to, who are Trump, Stephen Miller, armed protestors in state cap- itols, etc.

I have now been trying, daily, in the years that followed, and I am still not very good at it, and this inability has shaken me. I try so damn hard to sit in equanimity with the world and believe that everyone is doing their best, but I still cannot bring myself to it.

For the first time in my life, hate has creeped in, and I have come to believe that some people are perhaps not worth my acceptance or forgiveness.

But then after the unfriendly one, I think of the entire world—all the bees and rivers and people and art and kittens and red pandas and great cities and the triumph of the human spirit—and it's easy to wish them all to be peaceful, happy, and well.

So yes, spiritual practices are shaken and everything feels tilted. Friends, family, and I text our disbelief, our shock, our horror to one another. Everyone asks how everyone else is doing; the answer, of course, is "Not well."

I call my father so we can be aghast together.

Now, I love my father deeply, and he is one of the most brilliant men I've ever met. He also worked in risk management for much of his life and, thus, is phenomenal at not only sussing out every horrifying possibility but then describing each in what can sometimes feel like loving detail. Plus, in the grand tradition of fathers, I'm not sure I'd put emotional intelligence in his top-five competencies.

I had moved back and was living in my hometown of New Orleans in 2005 when Katrina hit. When it became clear my college wasn't going to reopen immediately poststorm, I flew to Oregon from wherever I'd evacuated to so I could be with my family.

My first night home, I'm sitting, shell-shocked, on the couch and talking about how awful it all is, and he decides out of nowhere that maybe I'm not sufficiently concerned about natural disasters.

"Well, you know, Sugar Bear, the *exact same thing* is going to happen here! Any day now!"

"Whaaaat?" I wailed, even as I knew Oregon is not really hurricane country. "What are you talking about?"

"Well, the thing is, the entire Pacific Northwest, and I mean *all* of it, has the earthquake, the Big One coming. I'm not kidding. It could happen *tomorrow*. It could happen *tonight*, right as we're talking! Now when it does, this town is gonna be history. It's just *done for*. This house is gonna slide downhill right into the lake. The entire neighborhood will! I mean, we'll all be crushed, but frankly I'm not sure you *want* to survive it, because . . ."

I pointed out to him that, as I was currently a week out from one city- and life-destroying natural disaster, I preferred to focus my energy on that for the moment and would contemplate the Big One later.

"Well, that's fine. I just want you to be prepared."

In this case, his awful thoughts turned out to be prophetic:

"I mean, the man is insane. He's not only a narcissist, he's a sociopath, and, I hate to say it, but he's just not bright. He's *reeeeeeeal* dim. And the problem is that when you have an executive who just isn't good at it and doesn't respect institutional knowledge, operations are one of the first things that break down, and they are *nearly impossible* to rebuild. Plus, what if he gets into insulting Kim Jong Un on Twitter and then we're all in a nuclear war? What if there is violence against groups of people by his scary, creepy followers? I just have no clue what's going to happen next."

What is the right thing to do here? Is going to work every day, coming home, walking the dog, etc., a dereliction of duty to my country? Should I be in the streets protesting, or should I try to stay as serene, capable, and ready as possible?

How is this real, and if it is real, what do I possibly begin to do with it?

A theory: Trump made me—and everyone, honestly, including his supporters—25 to 33 percent more crazy.* But some of us had a shorter sanity runway to begin with and thus began the descent. I feel unstable, disoriented, like I'm falling.

Then, I *fall* and begin the process of breaking myself.

✂

It was a few weeks after the election, and Sam's siblings had all come to town for a parent-free Christmas that involved lots of expensive beer and Portland strip clubs. I'm absolutely psyched to meet them, having already been on a top-notch text thread with them. When I do meet them, I immediately adore them and want them to like me. It's me, Sam, his brother, his two sisters, and his stupidly precious three-year-old niece, two days before Christmas.

"What should we do?" someone asks.

"Let's go to the mall a few blocks away and ice-skate," I say, and everyone congratulates me on this zany, unexpected idea.

Sam, of course, turns out to be an excellent ice skater and zips off handsomely. He does not look like he's moving much, and yet he is going so fast, leaning, smoothly putting one skate over the other, weaving gracefully through the thick crowd. Lucky for me, his two sisters are normal humans, pulling themselves along the wall like me while we get to know one another.

---

* This isn't just my theory; both studies and empirical evidence back it up. As a piece by John Harris and Sarah Zimmerman published in *POLITICO* magazine on October 12, 2018, put it: "The American Psychiatric Association in a May survey found that 39 percent of people said their anxiety level had risen over the previous year—and 56 percent were either 'extremely anxious' or 'somewhat anxious' about 'the impact of politics on daily life.' A 2017 study found two-thirds of Americans see the nation's future as a 'very or somewhat significant source of stress.'"

Then, Sam skates up to me, stops smartly, and offers a tutorial. I warily agree.

I should have known. My entire life, people have taken pity on me and thought they can improve my lot, she who doesn't know where her arms and legs are at a given moment, who moves like an octopus on land. They will just teach me, they think, how to shoot a basketball or run for more than 200 yards without wanting to die or swing a golf club without taking out a big clot of earth or whatever dumb physical arena they are good at and I am embarrassing myself in. They have seen my suffering, felt shamed on my behalf, and thought, *I can help.*

They cannot help me. No one can help me. My lack of athleticism is intractable, eternal. When I played one season of soccer, I was sarcastically nicknamed "Tiger" by the coach because I only moved when the ball came near me and I sprinted away from it. Being near the ball was dangerous because I was expected to kick it, or run, or do something that didn't involve staring at the sky and various trees. I played seventh-grade basketball and never, ever made a single basket—even in practice. When bowling, I have gotten gutter balls with the bumpers deployed, which shouldn't be possible. I fall down constantly and without warning, I am always covered in bruises of unknown provenance, and I've injured every single significant other by elbowing them in the face because, again, *I haven't the slightest idea of where my body is or what it's doing.*

And yet, ice-skating is working out quite well for me! I do have a tiny bit of grace and balance to my name; this reminds me of ballet or skiing. Soon, I'm moving quickly across the ice and, in my mind, looking extremely elegant. My God, I'm *really good at this!*

I have just enough time to contemplate how great an ice skater

I might have become, had this talent only been recognized earlier. Sure, not *Olympic* level and maybe even more of a speed skater than the figure skater type. Really, I *am* more of a figure skater, what with my love of sequined costumes and hatred of cardio, but then again I don't particularly like jumping, and I'm terrible at being a follow while ballroom dancing, so maybe in this case—

A child falls right in front of me, and my ice-skating dreams are shattered. As is my right elbow.

I manage to avoid falling on the child, but I come down on my wrist hard. I know immediately that my elbow is broken.

I knew this because I had broken the exact same part of the *other* elbow in the exact same way—well, falling on my wrist— eight years before. I was doing a little happy hop in an (un)Safeway parking lot to amuse the then-boyfriend.

I was 23, overdrawing-my-bank-account-every-month poor, and three days away from my health insurance starting. My boyfriend sat beside me, stroking my hair, begging me to go to the hospital, but I refused, opting instead to drink an entire bottle of Riesling and wait the 12 hours until a doctor's office opened.

I'd spent that night on a cheap couch in his apartment, my arm radiating pain throughout my entire body every time I tried to straighten my elbow. I would feel it in my gut and my teeth and my toes, a full-body spasm that was the only thing I could think of the same way all you can hear is a fire alarm. This was the same feeling, and, just as I had before, I decided this should be kept as quiet as possible.

I was asking for it! There I was, peacocking around, trying to look cool in front of Sam and his relatives. I'd skated too close to the sun, an Icarus who thought she was Nancy Kerrigan. God heard my self-aggrandizing thoughts and pushed me down on the ice. No, just kidding, that's not how God works. (I don't know how God works, but I have to assume that's not it. Right?)

Regardless, the wages of showboating are a fractured radial head, apparently. Sam skates up to me, freaked out. I do not want to make a fuss in front of his extremely nice and cool family, but I've really hurt myself and can't pretend to be okay. I always feel this way when I injure myself. It's sort of embarrassing, really, the fact that my bones have chosen to make this spectacle of themselves, falling down on their *one job* of providing structural integrity to my body. The least I can do is let everyone else continue to enjoy this road trip or wine-tasting or ice-skating without making it about me.

It's not just broken bones. I never, ever want to say I'm not okay; to do so feels like the most shameful thing imaginable. It's interrupting the peace of others to make things about myself. I never want to appear less than the 100 percent I am constantly trying to project. I am the Everything Is Fine Dog of injuries, pretending I'm not in horrific pain, because God, here I go again, being all *needy* and *dramatic* by breaking a bone!

I tell Sam, quietly, that my elbow is broken. He is at first incredulous because I'm being extremely quiet and calm. Could just he and I go to the urgent care nearby? Maybe he could tell his brother and sisters that I'm not feeling well? He is more interested in the potentially broken elbow than pretending everything is okay, which makes one of us.

Now everyone has joined us and is looking at me with horror. Not exactly the first impression I was hoping to make on his family. I have super-reasonable thoughts about what they will say about me:

"Oh, you met Kelly! What's she like?"

"So at first she seemed funny and cool . . . but then she broke her elbow for attention? I don't know. She's messy."

"Y'all should *definitely* keep skating!" I said, even though it was apparent no one is going to keep skating and the day is, in fact, ruined.

I make my way to the urgent care and in short order am in possession of a sling and a bunch of surprisingly powerful painkillers. Just like that, I don't have a right arm for six weeks or so; I am in a cast that starts at my armpit and ends at my fingertips.

Honestly, I would not and cannot endorse breaking one's dominant arm. It's not fun.

Here is a short list of things you cannot do with a full-arm cast:

1. Take a nice bath

2. Be any place besides your house, unless you can convince someone to drive you there or you're willing to wait for an extremely irregular bus in January

3. Go see your family or your friends

4. Cook much of anything

5. Paint

6. Embroider

7. Letter

8. Write a positive letter to someone

9. Type anything

10. Pick up your house (Honestly, this isn't the worst.)

11. Take a cute selfie without your dumb cast in it

12. Meditate without thinking about your elbow because it hurts all the time

13. Walk your dog because she's enormous and might pull you down on an icy sidewalk

14. Work on promoting your book that is coming out in two months, which is literally the only thing you're supposed to be doing right now

15. Really, any art except lucky paper stars and Perler trivets

16. Drive

17. Do your hair

18. Do your makeup

19. Masturbate

This is a fairly comprehensive list of my self-soothing activities, especially those last four, each of which are critical to my well-being.

I know my face sans makeup is not *that* bad. But as a redhead,

I have blond—and, therefore, invisible—eyelashes. Me without makeup is a very striking *Children of the Corn* or Maja in *Midsommar* effect, just a couple little squinty eyes set in pale, ruddy skin a bit like that of a piglet's. There is a reason that the makeupless redhead is a horror trope.

But what am I going to do, ask my friends to come over and apply eyeliner and mascara for me?

They are coming over, though, and bringing me stuff to eat, helping with Eleanor, and cheering me up. They've now met Sam, and we'll all hang out at my house, drinking hot mint tea with a splash of whiskey in it, piling in bed to watch a movie.

Carrie and her boyfriend are willing to drive me all over town. Emily comes by and is her loving, friendly cloud self, asking what I need, helping me nest, and not leaving until she knows I'm okay.

My mom and dad both come down to help me clean my house, put away my Christmas décor, and generally fuss over me—my father, in particular, is a bit of a hypochondriac, and we share a love of discussing our medical woes in great depth and boring detail.

But it still sucks! It really does! I am helpless and hapless. Nothing in my life functions as it did before because it turns out that having your dominant arm is pretty central to many human experiences. I have to coordinate rides to all my orthopedic appointments, or anytime I want to go anywhere that is not my house. I can't write or type; even using my cell phone is hard. I am pacing a *lot*.

I just want to be fine by myself, and I haven't been doing that. I've felt like a gaping wound of need for the past six months; at what point will people be exhausted by me? I'm tired of being fragile, vulnerable. I feel myself sinking down into something, and no amount of someone showing up to watch a movie with me can lessen the sensation.

During this time, I think of and yearn for my ex-husband. He was such a tender caretaker, so willing to help me gingerly out of a car, so patient when I'd once again hurt myself. He would come home with three kinds of soups, gently stroke my hair, and then make fun of me for the fact I had to lie on my stomach for weeks because I'd chipped my tailbone, but in a sweet, funny way.

I want to take care of people, not be taken care of. Being there in an emergency is my love language. If we're friends, I will be there in the middle of the night. I will invite you to move into my house while you're in the depths of this breakup. I will take you to the hospital and/or visit you when you're there because the thought of you being alone, scared, and in pain is unbearable to me. But I really, really, really, really don't want to have to ask you to do the same because what happens if I say, "I am truly hurting and need your help," and you're not there? It's the worst thing I can imagine.

Cast Decoration

I have now made it a tradition to decorate my casts. This stems from two things: one, it's like having a canvas to make art . . . on *yourself!* Two, if you're wearing a cast you have way, way more free time than usual.

Materials (all optional save the first):
- A cast, on yourself or another person
- Acrylic medium—SEE NOTE OF CAUTION!!!
- Sponge brushes
- Gold Liquid Leaf foil paint (It comes in a teeny jar that costs $9, and you have to shake it for hours, but it's worth it because nothing else actually looks like gold.)
- Some holographic nail tape that you bought maybe two years ago and have never been able to make stick to your fingernails
- Lotería cards
- Mod Podge

Instructions:

1. Decide that you don't like your full-arm cast. You've done the only fun thing with it—pounding it on various surfaces pain free, like it's a wooden hand—but now it bores you. It really needs a *certain something.*

2. Determine that you'd like it to have a texture like old-fashioned plaster casts, nice and smooth. Maybe you can even sand it.

3. Ask the one woman who is working at JOANN what you should use. She has *no earthly idea*, she says; she wouldn't know where to *begin* to start. No one has *ever* asked her this. But maybe some acrylic medium? That's what people use to add texture to a canvas. Maybe try that?

4. Why get it in clear when you could get it in navy? Gonna make a bold statement here.

5. Get all your other JOANN supplies at the same time because you can't drive and this is your one trip out.

6. You're also getting your hair washed at Supercuts! Washing your hair is one of the many, many, many, many, many things you cannot do for yourself. My gosh, that feels nice. Go home with clean hair.

7. Open the medium and stir it well. Goop a thick layer onto the cast with a Popsicle stick or butter knife, and try to smooth it out with a sponge brush. Note with a bit of sadness that this is not going to work, that you're still going to have that fiberglass waffle texture. Whatever, it's fine. The color is not your favorite. Again, it's fine.

8. Put down a paper towel that you can carefully rest your elbow on, keeping your wrist in the air. Wait for it to dry.

9. Wait.

10. Wait.

11. Wait.

12. Touch it.

13. How is it still wet?

14. Wait.

15. Wait.

16. Wait.

17. Okay, this is getting silly. Where is that jar?

18. Drying time: *72 hours.*

19. Fuck fuck fuck.

20. God, why did I go with *navy?* Why didn't I check the drying time? It seems like everything is dry to the touch within an hour; why not this?

21. Jesus Christ, *how am I going to sleep?*

22. Just going to have to wipe off as much as possible. Where are the paper towels?

23. The thick navy goop is mostly off. Okay. It can be gold. It can be gold and not that smooth. Shake up that paint forever, pour some into a small dish, and paint the whole thing, again using a sponge brush.

24. Wait for 30 minutes, which is a *reasonable amount of time.*

25. Yay! Back on track! Wind that holographic tape around it a million times. This looks nice! Leave it for a few days.

26. It could still use something. Something . . . like Lotería cards! I think there are some in the desk drawer. Go cut them up, carefully. Spread a thin layer of Mod Podge on the back of each card, and allow it to dry.

27. Apply another layer and then press the cards carefully to the cast.

28. When all of them are glued on, spread two generous layers of Mod Podge on top with a sponge brush. If ever you want to layer pieces of paper on something and have them stay, Mod Podge is your dude.

29. Pretend this thing on you is something you chose. It's so beautiful. Of *course* you chose it.

✂

And now it is New Year's Eve. Despite my injury, Sam and I have made plans to get away—we reserve a beautiful condo on the Oregon coast, right next to this huge cliff that sends up truly spectacular spray. We have good champagne, Dungeness crab, steak, and cheeses. The dogs are staying elsewhere. It's glorious, and a broken arm has in no way hindered the truly exceptional sex we are having.

As a south Louisianian, I subscribe to 18 million superstitions and am constantly assessing the air for any bad energies that may be afoot. This makes conducting life very difficult, as it is constantly sending me (mostly ill) omens. There is salt to be thrown over shoulders and bridges that one must cross with the breath held. There are certain things to eat on specific days, there are license plates whose digits must be rearranged and combined to make a year closest to our current one, and there are numbers on my odometer that must be observed (for palindromes, I get a wish; for hitting another thousand miles, there is a goal to be manifested).

One of these superstitions is that whatever you're doing at midnight on New Year's Eve determines the character of the year ahead; therefore, I take planning my New Year's Eve very seriously. Who am I with, where am I, how am I feeling? With the exception of NYE 2004, when I was throwing up Jäger as the clock struck midnight, I've been pretty successful in ensuring a smooth, happy transition.

At 9 p.m., Sam starts feeling sick to his stomach; the crab is suspected, and I am horrified on his behalf. I'd say I'm about 10 percent concerned that he's throwing up and 90 percent concerned about what this foretells for his 2017. Then, at 11:50 p.m., the bug hits me, and I am using my casted arm as a little bridge across the toilet that I can lean my forehead on as I vomit uncontrollably.

Realizing this will be my year-determining moment greatly compounds my already substantial misery. I try to adopt a serene outlook, but this is impossible when one is dry-heaving bile. I'm so sick that I can't even follow up on my *other* New Year's–related superstition about the importance of cooking and then eating black-eyed peas, greens, and cornbread on New Year's Day. Now not only will my year be puke-y, but I won't have any luck, money, or happiness.

I felt so in control and so independent only a few months ago. I had a brand-new life, I had a zippy little Miata, and I was falling in love. I felt strong in my decision to leave my marriage and, more importantly, strong in myself. And now I can't drive, I am terrified that fascism will creep across the country, I can do almost nothing by myself without enormous effort, and my body cannot handle more than a tablespoon of water without a violent reaction.

Maybe it had nothing to do with my superstition, but 2017 was indeed the equivalent of being violently sick in a beautiful beach house with someone you both love and barely know.

CHAPTER 4

No Apparent Distress

In Which I Break My Other Arm
and Meditate on the Nature of Independence
in a Time of Growing Darkness

Origami Lights for Sad-Naps

These charming little lanterns are a great way to illuminate your room during sad-naps! A sad-nap, of course, is when you get into bed when it is self-evidently a time you should not be in bed.

The goal of sad-naps is the sweet relief of sleep, which is preferable to not-sleep. Also, fun fact: You don't actually need to be sleeping to sad-nap! As soon as you crawl into that bed after telling your-self you won't, hey—you're sad-nappin', baby!!

Materials:

- Many matching or coordinating sheets of medium-sized origami paper, 5 or 6 inches (12.5 or 15cm) square (If you're an origami beginner, practice on some larger pieces first.)

• A strand of LED lights with small, cylindrical bulbs

A brief note: Origami diagrams can be pretty tough to follow if you're not used to them. I've done my best, but if you find yourself confused and frustrated, Google "origami balloon" and YouTube will have you covered.

Instructions:

1. Fold and then unfold the paper along the diagonals, horizontally, and vertically to make creases.

2. Fold it in half horizontally.

3. Pinch it just to the left of the vertical crease. Push down on the top-right edge so that side pooches out. Put your thumb in that opening, and squish the top-right edge down until what was the top-right corner is now nestled next to the bottom center point. Repeat on the other side. **Note:** If you are left-handed, reverse this process, perhaps? I don't know, I've never done origami left-handed. So I guess try both ways if it's not working out for you.

4. You now have four little points; two forward and two back. Fold each point up and to the center and then flip it over and do the other side, too.

5. Yay, four *new* points, and now it's shaped like a little diamond. This time, you're going to fold the east and west points to the

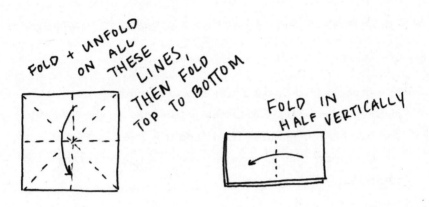

FOLD + UNFOLD ON ALL THESE LINES, THEN FOLD TOP TO BOTTOM

FOLD IN HALF VERTICALLY

SQUISH IT FLAT LIKE THIS. THEN, DO THE OTHER SIDE

FOLD EACH POINT UP, THEN FLIP IT OVER & REPEAT ON BACK

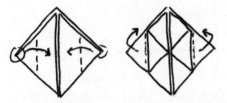

FOLD EDGES TO MIDDLE ON BOTH SIDES

TUCK TOP FLAPS DOWN INTO NEWLY FORMED POUCHES ON EACH SIDE

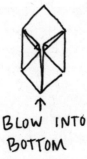

BLOW INTO BOTTOM

center. Do the front and then flip it over and do the ones on the back, too.

6. Now it looks kind of like a little top, or something. Look at the picture; it should be that. Grab the top point on the right side, and fold it straight down. Then—and this is not tricky, but it is, I guess, trickier than all the other steps thus far—fold the point southwest and then crease it.

7. Unfold it, open the little diagonal pouch, and fold it down inside.

8. Do that on the left side and then flip it over and do the front and back.

9. Now on the bottom, there is a small hole. Or opening. Sorry; every way I've tried to describe this sounds gross, and this next sentence won't help. Blow into that hole, carefully. Make sure your lips aren't too spitty when you do it, but do go for a nice seal if you can. **Note:** This is the most frustrating part of the process. You just have to try it a few times, and the first one will possibly, even probably, not inflate! Get back on that horse.

10. Grab your string of lights (I suggest Christmas ones!), and gently, carefully wiggle one of the lights into the hole. If it doesn't fit, you're going to need larger paper. If it does, hurrah!

11. Go back to the beginning and through the list again and again until you have a tiny balloon for every light. The balloons will diffuse the light and give off a soft glow. This is not the most

sophisticated of crafts, but it does looks pretty, and I feel like it would also make good sex lighting.

Caution: Be careful not to burn the house down with these, which is why I suggested LED lights. Plug in the lights for a while when you're there, and feel the balloons after, I don't know, 20 minutes. Make sure the lights are in no way hot to the touch. I honestly cannot imagine any reason in the world why this *would* burn your house down, but Jesus, I'd feel so bad. I have a weird and constant fear of house fires, and what if someone made these darling lights and ended up homeless as a result?

Addendum to the caution: This is a perfectly safe craft. I just get so afraid, and so maybe I should obsess about and voice aloud every terrifying thing that could conceivably happen as a result of my actions. God or the universe will then nod approvingly that I've really thought this through, and that dire consequence will not come to pass. This is logic *and* science, according to my brain.

✂

The first craft I ever remember mastering was the origami balloon. I was in second grade and had just received a book about origami for Christmas, having encountered it from the Japanese kids at my elementary school and finding it positively magical. You start with a flat, perfectly square, crisp piece of paper and end up with a tiny snail! What the heck?! It infused every piece of paper in the world with infinite possibility, using only your hands. I wanted in on this sorcery, and, because it's the tidiest craft possible, my mother was highly encouraging.

The first 14 balloons I made were tragic little things—squashy, misshapen, and uninflatable. And then, on the 15th one, I was as slow and precise as someone with an eight-year-old mind and pudgy lil' potato fingers could be. I bent my head low over the desk, slowly making each crease as precise as possible. At the end, it looked like the one in the book, and I tentatively blew into the bottom. To my shock and delight, there it was—a little rounded cube cupped in my hands. It was though I'd done magic without meaning to, like I closed my hands around a pebble, and when I opened them, a hummingbird flew out.

But then, as now, I am a hungry ghost who is always yearning for the next room, and so origami was only the first of approximately 146 crafts I have loved over the years. After origami would come friendship bracelets and plastic lace keychains, sculpting and pottery, watercolors and then acrylics, and then a very intense FIMO period that involved both millefiori beads and making tiny, tiny versions of food.

As a child, crafting and reading were the only things I really liked to do. I was one of those kids who, in the words of Julio Torres, just sort of waited for adulthood. I preferred the company of adults and found other children boring and confusing, although I'd always have one or two weirdo best friends who felt the exact same way.

But mostly I lived in my own quiet worlds of reading and crafting. Reading was perfect, as it transported me away from always being the new kid at school. (My family moved every year or so between New Orleans and Houston, so I was *always* the new kid.) Crafting went a step further: crafting took *everything* away, and it was just me and this little beautiful thing I was working on. Crafting quieted my little melancholy, ADHD mind.

It was my grandmother, Grannybarb, who taught me to craft.

She was—and is, death doesn't stop us!—my favorite person. When I would go visit her in this tiny Cajun town at the very bottom of the map, her small house was a place of wonder. Everywhere you looked were her little crafts—tiny watercolor faces, little stained-glass window hangings, sculptures from oven-baked clay, even these cozy knit slippers that everyone called bippies and were constantly badgering her to make. It felt as though the house itself was more alive because everywhere you looked, you'd see little things she had infused herself into, giving them souls. A card reminding her of her cardiologist appointment became a tiny painting of the flowers and peppers in her garden. I was in awe, and in love with, her art. One time, she gave me a little stained-glass box she had made, and I took it home and put it right in the middle of my dresser. When I was feeling extra sad or lonely, I would crack it open a tiny bit, stick my nose in, and breathe in the familiar scent of her house, her incense, and Granddaddy's cigarettes, and instantly felt safe and loved.

Her house was my favorite place in the world, because it had her and my granddaddy and everyone together at Christmas, playing poker and eating gumbo and drinking whiskey and laughing, while I sat under the kitchen table feeling so safe and loved. I remember, during one visit, gluing little purple gems onto a lacy, metal fan and then attaching tiny chains to make dangle earrings. She was so patient when she taught me to knit, again and again, even though I could never get it right.

She was so funny but so serene.

Morgan City

Louisiana

AKA GRANNY BARB'S HOUSE

"*Everyone does their * best *. SOME PEOPLE'S BEST IS shitty.*"
— GRANNY BARB

Her mantra, which I now have tattooed on my body, is "Everyone does their best; some people's best is shitty." She left Catholicism for Zen Buddhism (a unique choice in southern Louisiana!) and faithfully meditated for 50 years, going to weeklong silent retreats every year.

I was sitting by her bed the night before she died. She'd never really been willing to chat with me about Zen stuff, feeling strongly that it cannot be explained and had to be practiced, and she wouldn't do a good job of explaining it anyway. But I'd absorbed some things over the years and, for the last time, I looked to her for comfort.

"Are you excited about being reincarnated?" I asked.

"Hmmmmm. You know, I don't really have any thoughts on that."

I was slightly taken aback.

"Do you *think* you're gonna be reincarnated?"

"Again, you know, no real thoughts."

"Does that bother you?"

She looked amused.

"I mean, I don't see what difference it makes now."

Her kitchen table—the same one I sat under at Christmas, a 1950s blue Formica number—is now in my dining room, and I still hunch down over it as I craft and feel like she's nearby.

But back to the beginning of 2017. I was, at this time, truly adrift from my life as a writer. For years, I was the *Adulting* girl. I'd go to colleges and speak, feeling so fraudulent the whole time—and feeling even worse when I'd sign books afterward and people told me how much it meant to them.

But what had always felt like slight hypocrisy now felt like full-on fraud. Here I was, a clammy, weeping wound of need. What I had believed to be true about humans—that they are nice, that they care about one another, that they make good choices, that democracy is the best form of government—all felt on pretty shaky ground.

Plus, of course, my arm was broken and I couldn't do anything for myself, and my hair had been in French braids for a week and a half, a friend having offered after seeing I couldn't do anything to take care of my own hair.

Things seemed pretty awful, but lo, they were about to get much, much worse.

✂

It's January 20, 2017, and I'm streaming an inauguration whose very existence is an unsettling horror. My right arm still has a cast that starts at my fingers and ends in my armpit because my elbow is broken. My left arm is now strapped to my torso for the next six weeks after having been broken and dislocated. This makes turning the TV off difficult, because—and this may come as a real surprise to you if you've never lost use of both arms within three weeks of each other—everything is difficult.

On top of this, I am no longer good at speaking in entire sentences or remembering things that happened five minutes ago. This is upsetting. What's happening on the screen is upsetting. Everything is upsetting.

After an absolutely bananas speech from our new president,

George W. Bush leans forward toward Michelle Obama. "That was some weird shit," he whispers, and, when I read this the next day, for the first time in my life I agree with the man. This *is* some weird shit. *What is going on?*

Two Days Earlier

At 12:05 a.m. Sunday night, I come to. Maybe I was on the floor; I don't remember. But something is terribly, terribly wrong. My arm is radiating pain—but not the right one, with my giant cast. The other one.

I start texting anyone who might be awake and willing to help me—"Are you up? I need to go to the hospital"—and Carrie immediately says she's on her way.

Carrie arrives in her '90s Ford Ranger. I have no idea how it happened—I must've gone downstairs to let her in? Did she have a key? Did she have to help me down the stairs and out the door? Like so many details of this period, I don't remember. I'm sure she asked me what was going on, and I'm sure I told her I didn't know.

I had been told many times that the ER in the closest hospital is brutal, that if you're not going to bleed out in the 20 minutes it takes to get to Silverton, you should go there. But that's not what I'm thinking of in the middle of the night as alarm bells go off in my arm and brain.

When I arrive in the ER, a bewildering conversation begins.

"So what's going on?"

"Something is wrong with my arm. No, *not* the one with the cast; the other one."

"What happened?"

"I woke up like this."

"So you don't know what happened?"

"No. I don't. I don't."

I'm being seen by a physician's assistant. I remember her first and last name, I remember her face, and I will remember her for the rest of her life. I still fantasize about saying *very mean things* to her. I've tried so many times to set it down, but it doesn't work. When I was the most injured I'd ever been,* she was the only person who could have helped me, yet she chose not to.

She x-rays my elbow. Nothing. She pushes something that looks like an electric razor up and down my arm to search for blood clots. Nothing, although I scream when she gets toward the shoulder. I am trying to convey that something is very, very wrong, but I can't find the words I am searching for. She clearly thinks I am drug-seeking. Which, yeah, I'm sure lots and lots of people go to the ER seeking drugs because we have a god-awful opioid crisis and they're fighting a terrible addiction. This wasn't the case for me, but that doesn't stop her from treating me with contempt.

From the night's medical record:

> *She appears to be comfortable when not aware she is being observed, then begins to cry out in pain when I approach. The patient will be discharged home.*

She is speaking slowly at me. She doesn't think there is anything wrong with me, but if there is, my primary care doctor will find it when I have a follow-up visit with him.

---

* And believe me, there's been some competition.

I beg her not to discharge me. *Beg*, abjectly. All my previous stoicism in the face of my elbow break is gone. This pain is new. It's horrendous. It's all-encompassing. She is unmoved.

"I need you to follow up with your primary care doctor. You're going to need to see your primary care doctor."

When I passed patient in the hall, she appeared comfortable and was sitting in her stretcher in no apparent distress. As I pass, she becomes tearful and states, "I'm still in a lot of pain."

I'm crying—with snot—now: please, please, *please* let me have a second opinion. Let me see someone. Something is so wrong with me.

"You will not be getting a second opinion," she tells me.

"Well, what happens if I refuse to leave?"

Upon nurse's entry, patient dramatic and begins crying, saying she does "not feel comfortable leaving." Patient cries out in a loud shrill voice, states, "I am not leaving, I am in too much pain, something is wrong."

She will have no choice but to trespass me and then have me arrested. So now Carrie and I are walking out. She's seething. I am crying in frustration. And pain. There is so, so much pain. Carrie tells me later that there was a security guard following us through the halls, watching as she carefully loaded me into her truck.

No apparent distress noted on leaving, accompanied by female visitor.

I have to follow up with my doctor, but this is a weekend—a three-day weekend—and any visit is at least 48 hours away.

After what felt like 10 months, I go see my doctor. He asks whether they x-rayed my shoulder. They did not, no. He frowns and says, Surely they wouldn't have missed this, but just in case, and then sends me across town to get it x-rayed. That's when I discover that my shoulder is not only dislocated, but there is a chunk about the size of a walnut broken off the top of the humerus, now just sort of hanging out in the shoulder tissue. As it has been for days.

It can't just be popped back in now. I have to go back to—yep, you guessed it!!—good ol' No-Help Hospital and be put under general anesthesia. Carrie's mother, who recently retired from her nursing job in another department of that same hospital, comes with me to advocate. When I leave, my shoulder is back in its socket, but there's little clarity.

It's Emily who first notices that I am remembering nothing. Someone will bring my bag down from upstairs, for which I'll thank them sincerely. Thirty seconds pass, and I turn to them and say, "I'm sorry to ask, but is there any way you could get my bag from upstairs?" *Kelly, your bag is right there. On your lap.* Oh! Huh. Yeah . . .

My doctor is worried. He doesn't like any of this, not one bit. I shouldn't be breaking two limbs in three weeks. I shouldn't wake up with chunks of my shoulder bone bonking around in my body like a DVD player screensaver. I shouldn't have serious neurological issues that show up literally overnight.

The extremely dim silver lining here is that I've got a real-live mystery on my hands, and it's a corker! Unlike almost every other mystery that has ever landed in my lap, this one has actual stakes. Plus, I have no arms, so what the fuck else am I doing besides lying in bed trying to figure out how I got here?

I eagerly embark on *CSI: My Body* to get to the bottom of this mystery. Did I sleep on it wrong? No, the orthopedist said, this looks like I was in a car accident. Did I fall down the stairs and hit my head, erasing the memory of the incident? Nope, no bruises. Did someone break in to my house and dislocate my shoulder? Seems unlikely, as that is incredibly violent and weirdly specific.

Finally, I come to the only conclusion that makes any sense: a seizure! I had a goddamn seizure and fell out of my high bed with a stiff body onto a hardwood floor, presumably landing shoulder-first.

Seizures are *wild*. They are, in essence, little electrical storms inside your skull. Your brain waves, instead of looking like waves, look like crazy tangles of spikes.

Maybe it's poetic. Maybe during a seizure you think every thought you could ever have, remember every memory, move every muscle you own, understand the past, know the future—do it all, every single thing your brain has the potential for—even though you have no way of remembering it.

Or maybe, your sweet baby brain is, for a few minutes, Boggle cubes being shaken by a paint mixing machine.

I've actually seen my own brain waves, can you believe that? It was a rare treat I got in exchange for my first seizure in 2012. It's

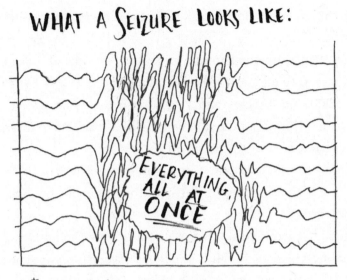

WHAT A SEIZURE LOOKS LIKE:

EVERYTHING, ALL AT ONCE

* Not scientific, but true.

called an EEG, which is short for electroencephalogram, and it measures electrical activity inside your head. Then, someone very smart looks over all the brainwaves to find seizure-like activity. It's so futuristic and makes you look like you are being mind-probed by an evil government in an action thriller!

It's the most fun medical procedure I've ever had. First, they attach dozens of tiny square pads to your scalp in different locations, which just feels like someone gently playing with your hair for 40 minutes. (Getting the glue out of your hair later is much less fun.) Then you do some good standard brain things, like count to 10 or talk about what day it is and where we are, move your right arm, etc.

My future former husband came with me for it, and he said it was beautiful—that when I'd move my arm, several of the waves would undulate faster, with higher crests, not in sync but together, and then slowly calm back down to their own slow, small ripples.

This time, I craned around and slowly sat up and looked at my own waves, thoughts, impulses, and unconscious acts—the things that make me myself—and I couldn't believe that people are so smart that they figured out how to make a machine that can show you these things.

Sadly, at that moment, my own brain was not in peak form. I'd had one seizure before, in 2012, and wrote about how my brain felt afterward.

It didn't feel like my brain anymore. My thoughts were like cold honey: so slow, so thick, so opaque. Everything was confusing.

It was the mental equivalent of cooking in someone else's kitchen. I spent all my time opening and closing cupboards, none of which had what I was looking for. Where are the measuring cups?

And now, I'm back. I can say yes or no, but anything else takes me a long time and keeps coming out wrong. To compensate, I make sure to say "yes" and "no" with a bright confidence. I want an onlooker to think, *Well, she has no arms, and doesn't remember what happened two minutes ago, but she* quickly *addresses questions with one-syllable answers. She seems good!*

I also mix up words, saying "fork" instead of "pen." I have the idea of a pen in my brain, I know just what it is and why I want it, but I open my mouth and something else comes out. Words are my whole deal! I know so many of them! But now not, apparently, "pen"! ☹

Most alarmingly, I'm not funny anymore. I mean, I have a sense of humor—someone says something funny, and I laugh, and then some part of my brain is like, "Okay, now you say something funny," but I couldn't grasp anything. I'd just reach and reach down a hole.

It's horrible to realize your habits and your traits and every memory you have—every Christmas and birthday cake and kiss— are all stored in a physical location that's not entirely secure.

Then there's the question of *why* I might have had a seizure. The last time there was a clear culprit—a medication I was on— but now there is no good reason, except for my I-have-been-cursed-by-a-wraith theory. So now my doctor feels like we should just go ahead and make sure it's not a brain tumor, particularly one that has metastasized into my bones.

I figured it probably wasn't really a brain tumor. The vast majority of seizures aren't caused by brain tumors. But my body is now a wreck, I have no arms, Trump is president—why not a brain tumor? I oscillate between sleeping for 12 hours and raw panic. I think about how, perhaps, I had completely missed something dark and ominous flourishing in my body, rotting it from the inside, just like I'd missed a very different darkness moving through America.

The world is absolutely bewildering, and I feel, physically and emotionally, like I have been hit by a sledgehammer. It's trauma on trauma, my body is broken, the country is broken, my marriage is broken, and I *still* have not sent all my thank-you notes from the wedding.

✂

Calming a Visceral Panic

So this is technically a craft for your brain because it only involves thinking, and there's not going to be anything to show for it except improved well-being. That said, like the crafts, there are things that I practice, again and again. And although they are hard at first and might not turn out, with practice, they really can make your brain a lovelier place to be.

Instructions:

1. Acknowledge your fear. Just sit next to it for a second, and look at it full-on. You can even say it out loud: "I'm so scared because I don't know what's wrong with my body, a lot of confusing things are happening, and I don't know if I have brain cancer."

2. Okay, so there it is, that's what you're afraid of. That thing will probably not happen, you can tell yourself, but on the other hand, it might. So how can we dwell together, me and this horrid possibility? How do I look it in the face and acknowledge that my fear is real but also that I cannot do anything about it right now?

3. Breathe in slowly, counting to five. Pause for a five count. Breathe out slowly, counting to five. Repeat this process five times.

4. Look, I know everyone tells you to breathe when you're having a panic attack, and it's *so fucking irritating*. I have personally

wanted to smack a certain former husband for just that on multiple occasions, but he was totally correct. You're not doing anything else productive right now, so go ahead and try that.

5. Say, slowly and out loud: "Right now I'm not in danger." Breathe in, pause, breathe out, and say: "I am not in danger right now. I am not in danger right now. I am not in danger right now. I am not in danger right now."

6. You don't have to believe it. You just have to say it.

✂

Once the possibility of a terminal disease is on the table, time starts moving very, very differently. It drips by, these four days between now and when I get my MRI. Intellectually, I was almost sure I didn't have a brain tumor that had spread to my bones. But maybe I did. Unthinkable things are happening. Why not this, too?

I have lots and lots and lots of time to think about brain tumors and also—in an *extremely theoretical and passing way*—that if I'm going to die, I should probably go take a certain someone out. Maybe I could get him alone without Secret Service if he thought I was going to sleep with him? I discuss this plan with Brooke as she drives me to get my MRI results, which involved hiding ordnance . . . somewhere, and being a Jezebel suicide bomber.*

One thing I learned from all of this is that I'd be so worthless against cancer. You read about people who just *really fucking fight it!* tooth and nail. They are fearless, they are tireless, they *never* give up, and they *never* surrender. Those people are really, really

---

*So, so, so darn hypothetically!

cool and admirable, and I am absolutely not one of them. Upon any reasonably sincere cancer diagnosis, I'm sure I'd skip all treatment and go do whatever I wanted until it was time to be dead, even if the cancer was the very-survivable kind.

Doctor: Hey, good to see you again! Some unfortunate news—the results came back, and I really do think we should remove that mole. We can actually schedule that today and get you back here in a week or so.

Me: Oh. Oh my God. Umm . . . I mean, I'll need some time to consider my options. I should . . . Can I have some privacy to call my family?

Doctor: I'm not sure there actually are that many options. It should only take an hour or so. I can check with Denise, but we might actually have time later this afternoon.

Me: The most important thing is quality of life. If it's my time, it's my time.

I will then clasp his hand in both of mine, giving him a moment to be in awe of my courageous and gracious spirit, and then turn on my heels and go have a *Y Tu Mamá También*–type adventure, which I have been meaning to do anyway.

Anyway, surprise surprise, I *don't* have a brain tumor, won't be assassinating the president,* and instead, just have a lot of physical therapy ahead of me. As for the seizure, I don't know. I'm

------

* Not that I would've anyway, haha!

not epileptic according to the 40 tiny probes that made visible my brain waves. I just seem to have a lower seizure threshold than most people, and sometimes these things happen and no one knows why.

For a little while, I'm animated by the thought of suing the hospital. That's right! I'll take the whole lot to court, even the security guard who followed me around through the hospital. I'll look that physician's assistant in the eyes, and *I will get justice.* Maybe someone will even go to *jail*! I'll then take my mom and Carrie's mom on a nice Alaskan cruise with my winnings.

Every friend who works as a doctor or nurse tells me that this is clear malpractice and I should sue. Every friend who is a lawyer tells me there is no point, that I would just be adding insult to injury. I'll lay out tens of thousands of dollars, go through awful cross-examinations, and then maybe walk away with some money in a year or two.

But I am so angry, I tell them. Someone should suffer because I have suffered. Maybe, they answer, but that sounds like a you problem.

So now I move out of the realm of exciting revenge fantasies and into the realm of "How am I even going to begin to do this?"—a far-less-satisfying realm.

I didn't need around-the-clock care without arms but, truly, I needed more help than I had since I was a toddler. Sam was around, sometimes—reasonable; as my mother points out, we've been dating for just over two months and he did *not* sign up for maybe-cancer. I had to remind myself that the six weeks I was without arms would account for nearly 50 percent of our relationship by the time it was done.

That said, it hurt that he was not often around when I needed help. I wanted—and, I guess, expected—him to be by my side, helping me, because that's exactly what I would've done for him. I can't help but think again of my ex-husband.

When I am in the depths of my impotent misery, I want to call my ex so badly, although of course I don't. I want him to be here with me, taking care of me. A mean voice in my head tells me that this is what happens, this is what I deserve, this is what God does to women who leave their husbands—pushes them down, breaks both their arms, and puts Donald Trump in the White House.

I hire one sweet middle-aged mother to walk Eleanor three times per week and another sweet middle-aged mother to come in once a week to clean and make food for me. I order implements from Amazon to help me shower and get out of bed.

Left arm capacities: The arm generally is useless, as it is bent and strapped, immobilized, to my torso. The hand itself is free, so I can hold, grasp, and manipulate things, if those things happen to be right next to my belly button.

Right arm capacities: This arm is in a cast that goes from my armpit to my fingers and is bent at an angle. So reaching for things involves a lot of new geometry for me; I have to be closer to what I'm reaching for *and* positioned in sometimes surprising ways to get the angles right. I really cannot reliably hold anything over my head—my weak little finger grasp is untrustworthy and limited in its capacity. It can hold something wide like a cup (unless it is filled with liquid, in which case, *too heavy!*) but not something like an eyeliner or a pencil.

If I want a glass of water, I swing my long-cast arm up to open the cupboard. I grasp the knob and then step back to pull it open. I step forward, grab the glass with the cast arm, back up a step or two, walk over, and put it down in the sink under the faucet. Step

back to close the cupboard and then walk over and turn the faucet on and off. Reposition to reach in the sink, grab the glass, and set it on the counter.

I open another cupboard and grab a straw, which I will set in the drink. Step back, close that cupboard, and return. Put the straw in my drink, bend my face over the counter, and grab the straw with my mouth.

If I want to drink anywhere besides the kitchen counter, I need to first clutch the water against my stomach with my left hand and then find another surface to set it on that I can lean my head over onto. Bedside tables work and, in a pinch, a coffee table will do, even though I know how stupid sitting with my legs wide and bending all the way over looks, like a sad little broken ostrich. Everything in my life is so stupid and frustrating.

And I'm in pain, all the time. I hurt a *lot*. My elbow hurts, my shoulder hurts, my abs hurt from trying to sit up without using my arms. My body hurts from lying in bed all day. If you've ever been hurt, all of a sudden, an opioid addiction starts to make a lot of sense.

It's hard to oversell how distracting and distressing it is to be in pain all the time. Your entire brain is dedicated to registering, minute by minute, the fact that something hurts. This is obvious if you've ever been through it and nearly impossible to grasp if you haven't.

Consider the experience of stubbing your toe. In the 45 seconds that follow, you are not a nice or smart or useful person. You are not effective, you are not accomplishing anything, and you could give a flying fuck about the really nice weekend that some dipshit (who is your best friend, when this trauma is not happening) experienced. There is one thing that exists in this universe, and that is your toe. All non-toe matters drop right off the radar.

It's that, but for *weeks*. Or months, or years. For many people, it's forever. But you know what's around, improving just about everything and sitting on your bedside table?

That's right! Kind-of heroin!

I have caught thousands of *extremely* lucky breaks in this life, and a huge one is that opioids fundamentally disagree with me. They make me itchy and nauseated and annoyed; I'm sure this biological quirk has saved me from profound heartache and/or death. If I liked opioids like I like cigarettes or whiskey or emotionally distant men with dark eyes, I would not be writing this book; I'd be dead.

I get why people are into 'em, though. On two occasions I got IV morphine, and it *ruled*. A cool fluid pushes into your veins, five seconds pass, and then your entire body relaxes and nothing concerns you. Contemplate the Holocaust, and you find yourself thinking, *Well, that was* really, really *bad. The worst, honestly. But it's been a long time, and I like to think we all learned a lot.** And then you nod off.

Those big white pills get you some of the way there. They don't eliminate the pain, but they give you enough space to think about something else for a bit. You still remember that your capacity as a human has shrunk to childlike levels—but is that really such a big deal? Who wants to feed themselves, anyway?

Thankfully, I had just read *Dreamland* by Sam Quinones, an incredible book about the opioid epidemic, and it convinced me that I wanted absolutely nothing to do with OxyContin. Instead, I turned to medical marijuana. I got my card and then talked with a lot of people who had also used it for pain management. Soon, I found myself with CBD tinctures that go under the tongue (the quickest relief), CBD rubs, CBD oil concentrates, and more. I also got a lot of tips on sitting with and breathing through the pain, which helped a great deal.

Also, a quick side note on CBD: for me, alone, it does nothing. It requires a tiny, tiny bit of THC to be psychoactive and bring me relief; I feel nothing when it's just CBD. Then again, all bodies are different!

It is also around this time that I start compulsively watching cable news. It does not escape me that, within the space of weeks, I have moved from a normal 30-something existence—Work! Friends! Grocery shopping! Dog walking! Sex!—to that of an octogenarian. Pills! Appointments! Visiting nurses! Confusion! *Morning Joe*!

---

*This is not a thought I have ever had when not heavily drugged. In fact, I regularly bring up the Holocaust to myself when I'm feeling too bullish on humanity.

But what else am I going to do? It's late January 2017, and I can no more ignore the news than I can ignore my lack of arms.

Do you remember how unhinged those first few weeks of the Trump era were? Before you developed the thick callus around your heart and could still be shocked and dismayed? I'd spent the 73 days between election and inauguration convincing myself that surely—surely!—it wouldn't be as bad as I imagined. Then it was worse.

I started doing nothing but watch MSNBC and CNN on the new giant TV I have purchased for this very purpose. In an effort to re-engage Sam, I asked him to help me find a deal on a nice TV. I know this sounds like an odd request, but Sam is a man who *lives* for deals. His favorites were always meat deals—he carefully tended his Safeway app and would somehow end up having them pay him $1.37 for a five-pound chuck roast.

When it comes to larger purchases, he researched each option meticulously, weighing the pros and cons with that brilliant brain of his, before making the exact right choice. If it were up to me, I'd just go to Best Buy and get whichever one had the most attractive bevel.

NEW ELDERLY ACCESSORIES

LOOFAH ON A STICK

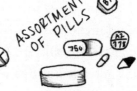

ASSORTMENT OF PILLS

CABLE NEWS

BREAKING
He's gonna kill us all. 100%. —🍊

He sourced and hung a big, beautiful screen that shows me, in ultra-high definition, all the fuckery that is afoot. I literally cannot turn away, but even if I'd had both arms, I probably wouldn't have.

I am not sure news should be legal. A unique position for a former reporter, and one that obviously I don't mean. But I think it can be really bad for us. Our brains evolved to know about the well-being of, like, 150 people. We humans are so, so good at noticing danger, and it activates us and alarms us, and now we know all the time about every single bit of humanity and every imaginable—plus many unimaginable—danger. I am just not sure we are built for that scale of bad information.

Plus, my news consumption has never been healthy. I've always checked every site, read every blog, needed it *all*, refreshing, refreshing, refreshing, an endless string of new, often alarming, discrete pieces of information.

That's why I got in the game in the first place; I wanted in on this knowledge, and I wanted to be able to create some myself. Maybe I'm just too goddamn nosy. Who am I, to think that I should know every single thing that happens to anyone the moment it happens?

Every day brings a punishing new level of depravity. Every day, more enraging, terrifying, utterly baffling things occur and unstitch my understanding of the world.

Emily and Carrie are right beside me, coming to visit and encouraging me to maybe not watch quite so much TV. Both had spent the day after Inauguration Day protesting, Carrie in D.C., and Emily here in Oregon. I wish so much I could be a part of this moment of humanity, and yet all I can do is lie in bed and feel afraid.

I am so mad at the capricious man in charge of the country,

and the baffling God in charge of my life. The country is broken, and I am broken, and even as I try to tell myself it won't be this way forever, I cannot assure myself it will get better.

But I try, so hard, anyway. This is, for me, the only reasonable reaction to pain and suffering. My instinct is to tell myself that it will get worse, but what I have to do instead is tell myself that it will not remain this way. I've never had a feeling forever, not once. If I've had a terrible day, I tell myself that no matter what, I never have to have that day again. If I'm hurting, I tell myself that it will not kill me, that nothing yet has killed me, even when it seemed like it could or would. As my friend Rachel would say, hope is a moral imperative.

It helps, for me, to repeat these thoughts as my fingers are re-peating a motion. It requires just enough focus to take me away from whatever I am precisely fretting about in the moment. Then, I can just tell myself again and again: this, too, shall pass, and probably faster than you think.

Even if things are going to get worse, which of course they always can, what's the point in telling yourself that? I face what-ever chaos is afoot with optimism because it sure beats the alter-native.

The elbow heals, and the cast comes off. Did you know that your muscles start atrophying within 24 hours of not using them? True story. So now I have a wonky little noodle arm flopping around and fingers that will not do as they're told. I need a couple months of physical therapy, not on my arm so much as my hand. I have to learn to write again, to do my own eyeliner without having to rest halfway because my arm is too weak to hold up for that long. But at least I have eyelashes.

The doctor decides that I don't need surgery on my shoulder—

oddly enough, the soft tissue hasn't sustained much damage, and my bones, despite what one might think, are healthy and have healed faster than expected.

Finally, I have both my arms back. But I'm not back to being myself. In fact, I'm drifting farther and farther out to sea.

CHAPTER 5

Scenes from a Breakdown

In Which I Just Cannot Get a Win

THE GOOD NEWS: I HAVE MY ARMS! GLORIOUS, GLORIOUS arms! With them, I can pick up a cup with the greatest of ease! I can close a door! Getting out of my bathtub doesn't involve lying my torso down on the edge and then just sort of carefully flopping out!

The bad news: I have slid into depression, which is surprisingly similar to having no arms. Getting myself a glass of water *would* be easier, if I had the will to get out of bed. Which I don't. Why bother? The only place worse than my bed, which is full of crumbs, as I have been taking all my meals there, is anywhere that is not my bed.

People who haven't been depressed assume it's sadness, but that's not it at all. It's not a feeling; it's the emotional flu, and it debilitates you. Things are going on around you, but you're too sick to care. You can kind of get it together sometimes, maybe go to the grocery store and stare at the Gatorade and put some into your basket, although even this decision is so confusing and hard. But then you're too tired to keep standing, you hurt, and you just can't walk much farther. So you go sit down on the pharmacy's blood-pressure-taking bench for a while and then cry because life is asking so much of you and you have no answers. By the time you get back home and into bed, you feel more tired than any human has ever been.

It is around now that every aspect of my life I'm in charge of starts to decline. Once, my mom said to me that she can always tell when I'm depressed because my house gets super messy. I agreed—there is absolutely no energy, in those moments, to clean up, and because I am sure I'm a disgusting pig person anyway, it seems much more on-brand to just keep the filth around me. This creates a positive-reinforcement loop: Am I a messy sack of shit whose coffee table reflects the garbage nature of her soul? Is that an old slice of ham? To both: yes.

Most arenas of my incapacity are invisible, although they cause real damage to others. I become a worse daughter, sister, partner, and friend. My work suffers, when I can do it at all. I'm not good at owning a dog; I'm not good at washing my hair; I'm not good at leaving the house; I'm not good at deciding how to spend my day.

Usually, I care about everything! So goddamn much! Politics! Art! Interior design! Appetizers! Dogs! Cats! Baby turtles! Fonts! Landscaping! People who walk too slowly! Paper clips, and whether they are gold! Costume jewelry of the 1960s! The ugliest thing we can find together in this Goodwill! Nothing in the world is too small or insignificant that I don't have the most strongly held opinions on it. One of my favorite qualities in a friend is the desire to parse our mutual love or hatred of every single thing in the universe together.

My godmother is the most hilarious and hyperbolic person I've ever met. Everything, to her, is holy or cursed, which is especially wonderful when she's describing, say, a T-shirt from L.L.Bean that did or didn't meet her expectations. It's either "the greatest thing in the *world*, I mean, now that I've *had* it, I'm mourning for the decades I *didn't* have it!" or "I swear to you that this God-forsaken garment was woven by *Satan himself*, to torture the good and the bad alike."

I dedicate myself constantly to someday achieving this level of criticism. So for me to just not care, to find everything equivalently awful, is to be estranged from myself.

The depression happened the first time when I was 15, during my first heartbreak, when the boy I loved broke up with me and started dating someone else. First, I was sad about him, but that quickly transitioned to not caring about anything, although not in the "fun, fearless female!" way.

This was the first time I began equating very inequivalent things. Maybe I will eat something today, or maybe I will drink water and then have two sugar-free Popsicles. Maybe I will drive home and park in the driveway, or maybe I will smash the car into the guardrail, but in a way that looks accidental. Maybe I will go to class tomorrow, or maybe we will all catch a break and the sun will explode.

So that's about where I was in the spring of 2017. I stop responding to text messages besides those from Sam, Emily, Carrie, and Margaret. People ask me how I'm doing and whether I'd like to get together, and this just makes me sadder.

I isolate because I can't think of anything except my own pain and self-disgust, and those who can't think of anyone but themselves aren't the best company. As you curl into your own misery, everyone else recedes into a shadowy background. It's the same as physical pain; there is so little room to care about anything else.

When people reach out, what would I say?

"Hey, girl! How are you? How are the arms? We need to get together soon!"

"Hi, Molly! I'm okay! I have my arms back (woo!), but also doing literally anything feels like slowly chewing then, with great effort, swallowing cardboard, and I don't *really* feel like being alive, lol. I don't think I can make any plans due to my busy schedule of lying in bed all day then drinking a bunch of whiskey late at night, alone, which sets me up nicely for the next day's bedstay. Kinda bummed I didn't have terminal cancer, tbh. Also I hear you're engaged, congrats!!!!"

Honestly, I felt I was doing everyone a favor, because the depressed are *such* a drag to hang with. We never make good jokes! We flake on plans! We don't really listen while you're talking!

Instead of telling people what's wrong, I just disappear. Better for them not to see me because then they might worry about me. Calls and texts go unanswered, which doesn't make people assume I'm unwell; it makes them assume I don't have time for them or think I'm too good for them. I find excuses not to go to anything (a lot of flus that winter). I send a ton of "Sorry!!! Just saw this now!" texts. I do get really good at using the Jimmy John's and Domino's apps, however; the better to remain on my couch and catatonically watch the news all day, embroidering with a thousand-yard stare.

I was in a perfect mindset for promoting something I worked on for years but now find utterly useless.

I'm supposed to be getting ready for the launch of my second book, a treatise on graciousness, kindness—the things I used to think were the most important things a human could do or be but now cannot bring myself to care about. Things, it seems, wide swaths of the country don't care about, either.

Two days after the election, I'd asked my editor if we could cancel the book, but no, that's not how this works. And, she says, maybe we will truly need this book more than ever. Maybe, I say hollowly, and besides, I'm contractually obligated.

The book was written from interviews with women I admire above all others. They were incredible, and had such beautiful thoughts to share with the world, and I feel like I failed them. The book was conceived and written in a world radically different than the one it was born into, and I leave my baby in a ditch.

The book was released to crickets, and so I go back inside my house and wait for the world to end. Which, honestly? Felt like it might. Hoped it might!

Now, I am alone in my house, ignoring my phone, capable of almost nothing—except crafts. I fill all the decorative bowls and gravy boats in my house with lucky paper stars. There are tens of thousands, in every color, plus prints, glitter paper, glow-in-the-dark paper, strips I cut out of the *Vanity Fair* magazines I cannot bring myself to read. I leave little origami frogs and snails around the house. I place them strategically so I can catch a glimpse of them as I'm washing dishes or taking a bath, an army of tiny cute things I cannot disappoint.

My Perler trivets and paint-by-numbers will not judge me, are not marveling at how far I've fallen in six months. They don't reflect my painful reality: only six months ago, I felt like I had leveled up, made the bravest decision I ever had made, and was ready to move into a future that belonged to me. Now, I wandered around a darkened house, drifted away from those who loved me, and couldn't handle tasks more complicated than placing one stitch and then another into a piece of cloth.

I mean, that year had everything—pet death! Human death! Weird health problems! Natural disaster!

I'm not going to try to put these things in chronological order or connect them neatly because that's not how I experienced them. It was just one insult and wound after another, blending together into a dark brown and red smear. I aged perhaps 10,000 years during this time. When it began, I was young and lovely; by the end, I was a UNESCO World Heritage site that 15-year-olds on school trips were sneaking away from to give each other hand jobs.

THE AUTHOR IN RUINS

What I couldn't see, as I experienced these things, was that this was all some very, very bad foreshadowing. Along with the incidents that can trigger depression—loss, catastrophizing, family history, and trauma—it was the first time I experienced an actionable desire to be free of all of it, free of my life, and began to walk toward something terribly dark.

Scenes from a Breakdown

SCENE ONE: LOSS

My beloved cat, Marigny Treme Brown-Gervais dies. She was 16, led a proud life, and left on her terms. There was nothing wrong with her that the vet could find; she was just tired of living, so she stopped drinking water.

I'd gotten her when I was 19, at the SPCA on Japonica Street in the Lower Ninth Ward. She moved with me through four states, lived with me in 10 apartments, and evacuated from hurricanes with me. The first time we had to evacuate, I'd only had her for about a week and was too poor to buy a cat carrier, so I wired two laundry baskets together, and she made the 18-hour journey to Houston in there, looking vaguely miffed the whole time. She was so small and feminine and beautiful; while she looked like every tabby cat in the world, she was also the prettiest. She was a ruthless hunter, had many unresolved mental health issues (she would be totally fine and then get a terrifying look in her eyes and bite me hard enough to draw blood) but was also a superlative cat. She loved when I propped my knees up in bed, and she could settle in underneath them, tucked in the covers. She greeted me with a quiet, "*Prrrrow!*" and a perked-up tail when I got home.

The reason you haven't heard about her until now is that she didn't spend the last year of her life with me—she was living with my former in-laws.

When my former husband and I adopted Eleanor, Marigny disappeared under a bed and would not reemerge for all the treats in the world. I'd go sit with her, in the upstairs guest bedroom, and she'd come poke her nose out and we'd have some time together before I had to go back to my life downstairs. I hated the idea of her spending the last year or two of her life in fear.

To my enormous relief, my mother-in-law also adored her, and we decided Marigny could live with her. When this decision was made, she was my new family I lived a mile away from and saw at least weekly, but things would, of course, change dramatically.

I have never stopped loving my mother-in-law, Mary. I still have dreams that she has forgiven me, that she loves me again. She was one of the most singular and special women I've ever met, and the entire topic of my second book, *Gracious*, was inspired by her. During all the book interviews, I felt like I was getting closer and closer to the answer of how to be like her. How to be selfless; how to be a domestic goddess; how to be someone who has dinner parties on sequential nights and makes it look easy; how to be cool and calm and collected but always above-and-beyond kind; how to show up for people; how to give and give and give, and, in doing these things, be a central part of your community, someone people know they can rely on.

Mary had already taken—and was loving—Marigny when my ex and I split. And of course, she continued to take phenomenal, loving care of her, and every day I felt awful about this. I abandoned my husband, I abandoned my cat, and there she was to pick up the pieces of the beings I'd loved and left.

She told me she adored Marigny, and it wasn't a hard thing to care for her, and I chose to believe her. We both loved that cat so. As Marigny's health declined, Mary kept me updated, and we planned a day for me to visit. When I arrived, Marigny was a shell of herself and didn't seem a bit interested in continuing this phase of her existence. She could barely walk but was doing everything she could to sneak away from me, which, to be fair, she did in the best of health, too.

And so Mary and I decided, together, that today would be the day. The vet couldn't see her until four, so we sat down and talked for the first time since I left her son.

I knew, in leaving, that I'd caused her so much pain and frustration and embarrassment, *plus* I'd left her beloved son heartbroken. I knew that divorce means loss, and not just of that one relationship; it billows out, and you end up losing so many more people than you'd guess. I did not, and don't, deserve her forgiveness or presence.

I could not turn back time and have Marigny as my cat again, and I couldn't turn back time and be someone Mary loved again. In one case, nothing but the cruelties of time are to blame. In the other, well, I know I did the right thing, but the choice I made still hurt many people I love. A divorce is a sort of social violence, one that will always explode farther and destroy so much more than you initially imagine.

It had always been so easy for us to chat, and so that day, we did it one last time. I told her I was happy (a lie, but what can one say?), we talked about the end of the marriage, we made each other laugh, and we both cried a lot as Marigny crept around the porch. I tried to imagine anything I could do or say that would make things okay between me and her, even though I knew such a thing didn't exist.

When I'd arrived in the morning, she'd been sewing some beautiful linen napkins for a shower she was going to throw for someone. She gave me some of the linen, and I started embroidering a shroud for Marigny with her full name—Marigny Treme Brown-Gervais—on it, and a tiny portrait of her face. When I was done, she took it, hemmed the edges beautifully, and pressed the whole thing.

Marigny Treme
Brown-Gervais

CAT FUNEREAL SHROUD

Around 2 p.m., my former husband came over to help dig a grave with his father, and once again, I was a part of this truly exceptional family I'd joined but just as quickly left. My ex and I snuck away, and I bummed some of his American Spirits, just like I always did. He put his arm around me, and I clung to him and buried my face in his armpit, that beautiful familiar smell that didn't belong to me anymore, as I sobbed.

At the appointed hour, Mary and I took Marigny to her vet, they lit the candle that indicated someone was saying goodbye, and I held Marigny while her breathing slowed and stopped. After, I went back, for the last time, to their beautiful yard. We wrapped the shroud around Marigny, nestled her little gray body into a white roasting pan, and buried her under a redwood tree.

And then, there was nothing left for me there, so I drove home, alone with my grief, while they held one another by the little grave.

SCENE TWO: CATASTROPHE

Summer is steadily rolling along, and now we are at the height of hurricane season. As a former New Orleanian who lived through the entire Hurricane Katrina rigmarole, I have some *feelings* about hurricanes. Images of buildings full of water, or an unexpectedly high tide, or even just seeing waves coming close to a building is enough to trigger it. I get this tight feeling in my chest that makes it hard to breathe, I feel a need to flee, and yet I'm stuck in place and silent. For instance, I had to leave the theater during *Aquaman* and *Ponyo* because those stories turned out to involve big waves, and if you've never had to explain feeling traumatized by a Miyazaki film for five-year-olds on a third date, you are missing out!*

---

* On PTSD.

I'm mostly better, now, and only think about it a couple times per week. But then came Hurricane Harvey! Harvey, bless its windy heart, managed to flood my childhood neighborhood in Houston, and once again I saw people canoeing down familiar streets and crying as they walked through their destroyed living rooms, and I wondered if that was actually Ashley Lawson's old house I just saw.

Meanwhile, the weather on the West Coast wasn't a hurricane, but it was quite malevolent, with a thick haze that made it nearly impossible to breathe outside and turned the sun into a flat red disk. It was wildfires, which seemed to be consuming every corner of the state. The TV reporters spent night after night making sad faces and pointing at maps of Oregon speckled with glowing orange blobs. Those blobs always seemed to be getting bigger, sometimes even merging with one another, and I spent a lot of time thinking about baby deer and owls and big old special trees and places that were someone's very favorite, all now gone forever.

A collectively painful wildfire was burning in the Columbia River Gorge, which is the most stunning place in Oregon. Everyone thinks so. I don't even like nature, and I love it. It's a miles-wide canyon where the Columbia River cuts through the Cascade Mountain Range; I drive every single visitor to Oregon I have to see it because I can almost guarantee they've seen nothing like it before. Now, because some 15-year-old *dipshit* from Vancouver, Washington, was tossing firecrackers around to *show off to his dipshit friends*, the whole thing may never be the same in our lifetimes. Sam's very favorite place in the world was a backcountry trail that is being consumed at that very moment, and he is stricken, sometimes seeming on the verge of tears.

A thin layer of ash that used to be trees and wildlife is covering everything; I thought about sweeping it off my car and porch but figured, why bother?

Hurricane Maria hits Puerto Rico, which is my second-favorite place in the United States besides New Orleans, and while people are dying (more than on 9/11!), that man is throwing paper towels at them, and once again nothing is okay. The planet is dying, and Black and Brown people are being left to die by the government, and everyone is carrying on as though things are just fine.

I think if I'd been in a normal state of mind, these things would still be horrifying, but in my current state, I take it as further evidence that the world was quickly coming to an end, and I spend the days crying with frustration and powerlessness.

SCENE THREE: DEATH

In the midst of all this, my grandmother dies. Not Grannybarb; the one on the other side of the family, the dark, Southern Gothic, semiestranged part. Her life was so hard, and she herself was so miserable, being quite familiar herself with depressive episodes, although to my knowledge, she usually relied on Jesus and not medication for her relief.

She'd been, for a short time in her life, fabulously wealthy, with a husband in oil and the ability to buy the Cadillac she'd dreamt of since she was a dirt-poor girl in South Carolina. She had that life for maybe four or five years and then oil crashed and her husband died of a heart attack, leaving her with $800,000 in medical debt. And that was 1989.

So for 30 years, she missed her husband and went back to barely subsisting, with the help of my dad, and had untreated depression and arthritis of the spine and a lot of other dark stuff that I'm not going to unpack here. Whenever I tried to talk to her and cheer her up, she spoke of going to Heaven to be with Granddaddy, and I said how nice that would be, and that I love her, and I hope she wasn't hurting too much.

I wanted, so badly, to give her peace, to bring her joy, but I couldn't. When she dies, a couple days after Marigny, I don't cry but am instead flooded with relief.

SCENE FOUR: WHO AM I?

Among all this, I manage to gain a full 50 percent of my body weight—and not a healthy or necessary gain. Honestly, my body does a lot of things well, and one of them is *immediately* gaining a lot of weight during times of societal disturbances. This makes all sorts of sense from an evolutionary standpoint, but to date, it hasn't helped with Hurricane Katrina, Trump, or coronavirus. Admire the effort, though.

I am now moving through the world in a very different way emotionally, mentally, and physically. I've become invisible to men, which is just fine with me, but I can't fit into any of my clothing and cannot dress like myself anymore. I put all my favorite dresses down in the basement, so they won't mock me, and I stop looking in mirrors because I don't really recognize the person who looks back.

It was just one more way of feeling that life had become unrecognizable from a year before. Maybe there was continuous occupation of the same cells, but I was no longer me. Things inside me had been turned off; bits of my internal architecture sagged. It felt like a wing of me had collapsed, and now nothing was structurally sound.

Sam, to his credit, doesn't mind. We talk about eating healthy, we talk about going on long walks together, we talk about so many things that I know would help, not with the weight but with everything, and yet I cannot get it together to do any of them.

SCENE FIVE: IDEATION

I lie in bed one night and pull a neck scarf tight around my neck. I don't really mean it; I just want some sensation other than this black, numb cloud that hangs around me. After a few minutes, I get out of bed and wake up Brooke, and then a bit later, Sam, and tell them what happened.

Much later, Brooke told me her memories of that night:

"That day, I was asleep in bed with Ben. I remember hearing you crying. I see you, and your mascara is gathering below your eyes. I can't tell if you're drunk. You tell me about what you'd done, and you start to tell me that you had tightened the scarf around your neck tighter and tighter. You kept saying that the people around you would be sad but you made everyone's lives worse. I told you that I would help you find a therapist. You told me that you wanted to go talk to Sam, and that you were going to take a bath."

She continued: "I remember waking up Sam, or maybe I just remember hearing him. I remember him sounding angry—'Jesus

Christ, what is it?'—and then feeling so angry that he would talk to you like that when you were struggling. I stayed up and called people, looked up websites for therapists. I didn't go back to sleep. I could hear you crying in the bath. I texted you a list of potential therapists.

"The next day, I kept texting and calling you, because I hadn't heard from you since you said you were going to take a bath and I was afraid that you were dead. I couldn't focus at work. I started texting Sam, and he eventually sent me a message saying that he was scared, but that you were okay.

"When I saw you, I was mad—I was mad about how fine you seemed, as if nothing had happened. 'I'm sorry that you're upset; you're not helping me with this,' you said. I carried so much rage after that—as if I was upset about my role as a character in your life, and not deeply afraid of what you might do to yourself."

Years later, reading this, I am so ashamed. How could I possibly have said something like that to the person in my life most dedicated to getting me help? This is how through the looking glass I was: I remember thinking Brooke felt she *had* to do that for me, and she surely didn't want to but felt obligated. I remember thinking that if I pretended nothing had happened, she could just move on and I wouldn't, once again, be causing problems for everyone.

And here, dear reader, I will tell you something that perhaps I should've told you at the very beginning of the book: I don't always remember the truly scary things clearly. I am not always a reliable narrator because I always put the best spin on things. I fill in the gaps with more palatable details, retcon them into something that isn't quite so gutting to look at. There's a debate about whether this is healthy, but I believe this is what has helped me survive.

But this action was a very, very bad sign. And for me, it was a new one. Despite my sometimes-casual attachment to being alive, I'd never, ever done anything like this. Suicide had always been unthinkable to me. I've lost friends to it, and I know that it's a shrapnel bomb that goes off and tears everyone close to you apart—the more they love you, the more you are consigning them to a life of complicated, unresolvable grief. Normal me would be horrified by this, but then again, normal me would not be cool with any of this.

Despite my desperate desire to move on from this and pretend nothing happened, I know I need help. I try, sometimes, to call therapists. A few days will go by, they'll call me back, and I'll never return their calls. I simply do not have any capacity; I am empty and ravenous and rattling inside.

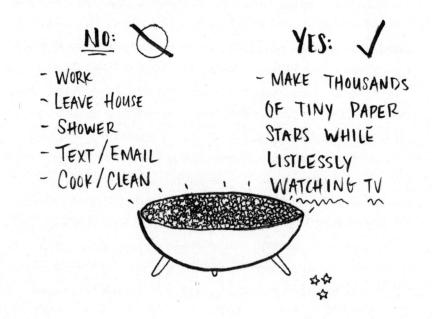

NO: ⊘
- WORK
- LEAVE HOUSE
- SHOWER
- TEXT/EMAIL
- COOK/CLEAN

YES: ✓
- MAKE THOUSANDS OF TINY PAPER STARS WHILE LISTLESSLY WATCHING TV

SCENE SIX: THE FIGHTS

Sam and I are arguing, all the time, about what, I cannot tell you. Legitimately, I cannot now remember what even one of our fights was about. Really, they weren't about anything other than the fact that we were both depressive people who were, at that moment, doing quite poorly. We both needed support that the other could not give. The scene repeats again and again, and once more, I find myself in a relationship where someone often gets mad at my behavior in ways I don't understand.

SCENE SEVEN: MY DAD

My dad had something in his throat that had been bothering him for a while, but he didn't think much about it. Then, naturally, it turned out to be throat cancer.

He had a very, very good prognosis, but he needed radiation, chemotherapy, and a feeding tube. He is scared, and I'm pretending to be very confident when I'm on the phone with him. "It's going to be okay! Just two really shitty months! You can do it! You'll move through it!" Meanwhile, I know how grueling cancer treatment is, and that it will not just be two months, but how can we bear to approach more suffering than that?

We bicker about little things like whether he will please just let me get him a recliner so he can sit upright and eat in comfort (he balks, having held a never-explained lifelong hatred of them but eventually agrees) and whether my little sister can come make him healthy smoothies (which, again, he is anti for not-entirely-clear reasons). I am rearranging my schedule to try to figure out how I can take care of him and be in the house because I know what it's like to be fragile and incapable in a way I'm not sure he does.

My father has always looked great for his age. He's in his 70s but could pass for a decade younger. But now, all of a sudden, he's showing his years, and he is so, so tired. This is a man who has run several times a week since the 1960s, and now he cannot get out of a chair.

During this time, only three things—besides crafting—bring me pleasure.

The first is my friends and the little adventures we have together. Going to a kooky beach house, whose entire aesthetic was early 1990s *The Rainbow Fish*/orcas, and watching Eleanor and Sam's dog run across the dunes together. Making costumes for this tiny Burning Man–ish party outside Salem that's held every June in a beautiful forest canyon. Having people camp in the backyard for a combination Carrie's 30th Birthday/Total Solar Eclipse weekend. My father shows up about six hours earlier than we'd discussed, just when some people (not naming names, but it wasn't me) are *really* starting to feel the mushrooms, so that was fun.

The second is Sam. It's true that Sam and I fight. A *lot*. (This was becoming a pattern in my intimate relationships.) But we love each other fiercely and unstoppably, and we each work so hard to keep the other one afloat. Sam always helps me keep the house together. In turn, I listen to him, comfort him, and calm him. Plus, no matter how bad things got, we have that ding-dang chemistry. Sex is truly one of the only life-affirming activities I have at that moment. It makes me feel alive and beautiful and powerful but also safe, protected, and loved.* For the first time in my life, I feel like I could be truly open with someone about sexuality without shame or judgment; I know he instead treasures this

---

* Plus, Sam was *great* at it.

part of me. While everything around us seems to be actively rotting, this is something vital and alive that helps carry me, and us, through.

The third . . . and I'm not gonna say *most* important, but . . . is *Bob's Burgers*. This is how much I love *Bob's Burgers*: for a while, I was planning to dedicate this book to its creator, Loren Bouchard, and John Roberts, who voices my favorite character, but decided that would be too much. Writing it out here, though? Very normal and cool.

Bob's is gentle, funny, and beautiful. It's rare to find something that makes me laugh so hard *and* makes me feel better. Yet there it is, the story of a kind, slightly insane family who truly love and support one another, and I can lie on the couch and consume it nonstop. You can tell that the writers love the characters, and they put those characters in a much better world than the one we live in—a world where everyone is ultimately celebrated instead of judged.

I'd been told for years to watch it and would watch an episode and be like, yeah, okay, that's fine. But somehow—I can't remember if it was Brooke or Carrie, but the whole house loved it—I got on a major kick. I watched all eight seasons. And then I watched them again. And again. I fell asleep to them, I woke up to them, I didn't watch so much as listen to it in the background while crafting or, more often, playing dumb cell phone games. I love all of them, each character, in different ways, although Linda is my favorite.

It was probably the gentlest environment I could insert myself into, and to this day, it still gives me great peace.

More than a year later, when things were darker than I could have ever imagined, I was by myself in 7-Eleven on my birthday.

A bunch of personalized keychains caught my eye, and I decided to buy myself a "LINDA" as a present, hoping it would help me spend my 34th year manifesting Linda Belcher energy within myself. She isn't real, but what she means is—someone who spills love everywhere; who breaks into silly songs; who, in her words, doesn't get drunk but has *fun*; and someone who is always surrounded by her most beloved people to whom she can give her best.

Nail Polish Dragon Eggs

This is a wonderful craft for the agoraphobic compulsive TV watcher. (Although a perfectly healthy person would also enjoy it!) It's easy to do and hard to mess up, but it takes a while, and in parts you have to be painstaking or willing to backtrack. Because of this, it gives you a tremendous sense of accomplishment. When you're done, you have this lovely, heavy, soothing thing to run your nails over or, for the true sensualist, rub up against your face.

These instructions are adapted from the Dragon Egg Tutorial, which can be found at polishthydragoneggs.weebly.com, an offspring of the Polish Thy Dragon Eggs Facebook group.

Materials:

- Thumbtacks—a *lot* of them! You need the flat, metal-head kind, and you're buying in bulk. For a 4⅞ × 3½-inch (12.4 × 8.9cm) foam egg, which is about the size of a large lemon, you need 900 tacks. Other sizes and tack estimates are given on the tutorial webpage.
- Something to stick your tacks into as you paint them—a giant Styrofoam sheet could work, but so could cardboard. If your tacks poke through the other side, make sure you set another piece of cardboard down under them.
- Nail polish! You want a good, pretty base color (sparkly blues,

greens, reds, etc., work well; holograms and chrome polishes are also great), and, if you're me, you're gonna want a glitter color, plus a topcoat to make them nice and shiny. But you could also go with baby blue and white flecks to make a robin's egg! Please note that you should *not* use your favorite, limited-edition polish on this because it might easily take up half the bottle (and will dry your polish out a bit from being open so long). Cheap is just fine here, and that goes for the top coat as well.

• A foam egg, available at craft stores and online.

• Some glue to hold the last few tacks in place. Foam glue or E6000 would work.

Instructions:

1. Push all those tacks into your tack-holding material of choice, but not all the way down—you want to be able to paint the edges.

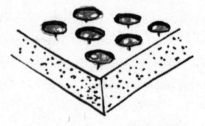

2. Paint them all with your base color—again, making sure you get the edges.

3. Let the polish dry thoroughly between coats. It's not dry if you can dent it with a fingernail.

4. If necessary (and it probably will be), do a second base coat and then let that dry.

5. If you want to add glitter polish, this is the time! Let dry.

6. Top coat those tacks. Let them dry.

7. Y'know what, just let everything dry overnight.

8. The next day, grab that foam egg. You're going to put the first thumbtack at the very center of the rounder end. Then, you're going to put another tack in so it slightly overlaps the first.

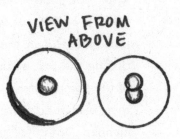

VIEW FROM ABOVE

9. Going in a clockwise direction, make a circle of six tacks around the first one, with each tack overlapping the one "below" it and to the left of it.

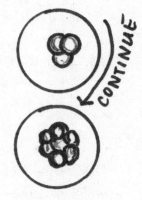

CONTINUE

10. Now you're going to make a circle around that row, again, moving clockwise. Put each tack in the V formed by the tacks above it.

11. Try very, very hard to keep the circles even, so you're not getting higher on one side of the egg but rather working in a straight line. Rachel, the founder of the Facebook group who can be found on Instagram at PolishedNails And-DragonScales, said that if you find it getting wonky, you should backtrack. "Don't feel bad removing them from the egg and starting over," she said. "That way, you get to have the practice without having to paint a bunch more tacks."

12. After you pass the thickest part and the egg begins to narrow, the tack circles will obviously get smaller.

13. When you get to the final ring at the top of the egg, you'll need that glue. Put in the tacks, including the one at the very top of the point that will hold everything else in, to make sure you've planned correctly. Then take them back out, spread a thin layer of glue on the egg itself, and push the tacks back in.

TOP OF EGG

LAST ONE GOES IN "X"

14. Congratulations! You've got a delightful thing to hold, click your fingernails against, or rub on your face!

✂

Despite the precarious state of my emotional health, 2017 ends on a great note—a New Year's Eve that was 10,000 times better than the last. Honestly, even if you're not in a deep depression, I can't recommend a small New Year's dinner party at your house highly enough. It's truly the only reasonable thing to do with the night.

So, as I always do when I'm throwing a party, I go all out. The house is fully decorated, I'm busting out my fanciest place settings, I've made gumbo with meats I smuggled

back from New Orleans, and I've embroidered everyone a tiny favor.

The usual gang plus a few others are at my house, and we are having a ball. This was the era of the online gaming sensation HQ Trivia, and we all tried to participate in the much-hyped million-dollar round. It was supposed to happen right at midnight Eastern Time, except it was a complete fiasco. So many people logged on that the scoring system crashed—and there was the host, poor Scott, live on camera, hearing from millions of angry people who had missed their New Year's moment for this. My personal favorite comment was "SCOTT IS SCUFFED." We all immediately took to this, noting for months later everyone and everything that was scuffed.

Carrie's cousin, a ceramics artist, was there and gave me a small piece she'd made as a hostess gift. We lit candles and did Tarot for the year ahead, and, after every terrible thing that happened that year, I felt enormous waves of gratitude to be with them. I'd picked the song to play at midnight—"No Bad Vibez" by Rich White Ladies, which is two best friends rapping about how they're conquering the world.

We scream "Happy New Year!" and Carrie and I dance. The world is awful, but at least I am surrounded by the people I love most in the world, and, in this moment, I feel the tiniest bit of optimism.

CHAPTER 6

A Fertile Time

In Which I Seek the Meaning of Family and Find Some Truly Terrible Ideas

MY LITTLE HOME, FULL OF FRIENDS, FEELS LIKE A MIRACU-lous occurrence in my 30s, when so many friends are married, or, even more dauntingly, have children. It began happening in my mid-20s, reaching terminal velocity at age 33: one by one, my friends were raptured into motherhood.

I truly do mean raptured. They live in a new state of bliss (but also insanity and tiredness and spit-up) with an entirely new daily experience, new values, and new desires.

They are part of a club, one with a seemingly endless stream of talk about nursing and childcare, one that goes on long weekends at a lake or whatever, all their children playing adorably in the water together. A club that the childless cannot be part of, no matter how much we might wish to be.

When my friends tell me they're pregnant, I am really delighted for them . . . but a small part of me is quite sad because that friendship cannot continue to exist as we have known it. It's a unilateral decision on their part (as, um, it should and must be) that radically alters the quality and quantity of friendship available. A close friend who has just as much time and energy for you as they did prebaby is someone who is probably neglecting their child.

It separates you. Your friends are just as important to you, but you have been knocked down several notches on their list of priorities. They have moved away, to someplace they say is much, much better—so great, in fact, that you could never understand it unless you yourself sold off all your belongings and moved there, too. From where you're sitting, the new town looks exhausting and unrelenting, but they say it's worth it. They wish they could explain it, but there are just no words. Meanwhile, you're still back in the old town, which you *thought* you really liked, until all your friends start moving away.

Of course, I am on one side of this and have not experienced the other. I know new mothers often feel a great loss of sense of self, an invisibility. I know they are having their own very complicated feelings on the subject. But they so rarely express them, and when they do, they feel a need to immediately double back on themselves, perhaps so Fate doesn't hear them talking carelessly.

It's hard to articulate this friendship loss because I'm not *supposed* to feel this way. It's really, really selfish. A baby is a beautiful and joyful thing, and perhaps the biggest, most important step my friends have ever taken to experience their humanity to its very fullest.

They, quite reasonably, are extremely wrapped up in this new pursuit. They want to talk to people who know what they're going through, not people who find the pregnancy and childbirth processes kind of disgusting. Which . . . come on, *they are*.

There are many miraculous but also objectively horrifying things happening to a pregnant woman's body. A friend who had recently given birth could tell me her body was doing literally *anything*, and I would believe her. There is no level of body horror I would not nod at, working hard to keep my face in a calm, neutral expression.

"Yeah, around week six the nipples actually develop tiny mouths and start humming 'Toxic' by Britney Spears if your baby feels bored or gassy. Even if your baby is miles away, the nipples just *know*. At 10 a.m., a smooth piece of obsidian pops out of my vagina, and I immediately eat it because my body *craves* volcanic glass. I'm actually developing a *mole pattern* on my back that portends Trevin's future SAT scores. It's *amazing!*"

"I'M TELLING YOU— EVERY MORNING! IT'S LIKE CLOCKWORK!"

Your friend isn't the same friend she was. She's a mom, and she *should* be a mom. She should take on this insane, heartbreaking, beautiful task. She *should* shape the future. She *should* throw everything she's got at the cause, and continue to throw as hard as she can even when totally depleted. She shouldn't have time for you.

Yet . . . it sucks that she doesn't have time for you.

This is all complicated by the fact that I don't want children, except when I do. This lends a real "Am I sad because I feel like I've lost that version of our friendship, or am I a jealous, bitter little bean?" cloudiness to the enterprise.

It's probably a 72/25 no to babies for me, except when I think about growing old and dying alone . . . or the fact that in roughly seven years, this won't be a choice anymore. Then, the pendulum swings hard in the other direction, and I start to panic a bit. This happens maybe once or twice per month, although as I get older, I think of it less and less.

I definitely don't want a baby; they are loud and boring and exhausting. I'm not even sure I want a child. I love spending time with other people's children and then I love handing them back and departing in a tiny, impractical convertible. Looking at the parents of a child under six, I nearly always feel the deepest relief that it's them, not me. I can't imagine something that not only needs me all the time but also needs me to be my best self.

Almost none of what makes me happiest is compatible with parenthood. I love sleeping in, taking a laze, soaking in absurdly long baths, lolling around in UGGs, watching *Vanderpump Rules*, and fucking off on a road trip or to New York or even to another country if I get a good deal on tickets.

There's also the question of submitting your body to the process. I like my figure, my boobs, my tummy, my long hair. As someone who historically has not always been okay with my body but cherishes it now, it's frustrating to think of it all changing immediately and permanently. I worry about having a husband who doesn't want to fuck me or, much more likely, a me who doesn't feel sexy or sexual anymore.

Then, there's money! I like to spend mine on myself (and friends and family), on going out to eat, or on fancy cheese or wine or costumes off Etsy for my giant dog, or art supplies or jewelry from estate sales. I don't want to spend it

FARMER'S MARKETS: ABSOLUTELY NOT.

on organic farmer's market produce that I then cook into a child-friendly recipe.

Having a child, by necessity, forces you into a new world, one that is less about friends and Bravolebrities and perhaps people and things in general that are not your baby. And, when my depression is at bay, I love the world I am in.

I'm not even sure I *want* to bring someone into this world right now. One of my very best friends gave birth a couple days after Trump was elected, and I can't imagine how that felt. It was a bewildering, terrifying world, and my opinion of it has not improved since. I don't know what the next 100 years will hold, but having already gone through a climate-related nightmare (Hurricane Katrina), I'm not sure it's going to be super great.

But then again, sometimes I do want motherhood.

I want to patiently explain why the sky is blue and why cats don't talk and why we say "Excuse me" when we are in someone else's way. I want to teach a small human what a real apology sounds like and how you treat people you don't like and why one shouldn't interrupt or talk with their mouth full. I want to have Christmas traditions; I want to be the Easter Bunny; I want to go to the beach for a week every summer with some other parent-friends.

I want something actually important to focus on so I'm not dwelling in my own small bullshit all the time. I want to be grown-up and selfless in a way it seems the childless don't always achieve. I want to care about something more than I care about myself. I want to pour much of my time into the staggering, insane project of trying to help someone become a happy version of themselves, to let them know they are always loved.

I want to build a cohesive unit that continues to grow without me. I'd like someone who hopefully will love me even when I am disgusting and infirm, so I will not have to charm my nurses in order to trick someone into talking to me. In the run-up to oblivion, doesn't it seem preferable to have people who are fond of you, to be able to gaze upon what will remain of you when you're gone?

These are somewhat insane reasons to bring a human into a broken, worsening world. One should not create life based on vague anxieties about what could possibly happen 60 years from now. I hate the idea of dying in a hospital bed anyway. Fingers crossed so tight that I'll be hit by a bus as a spry 72-year-old at the peak of her eccentricity, and that will be that.

But motherhood is arguably *the* human experience, and I *adore* human experiences. As someone who is obsessed with love and the chemicals my brain makes around it, this is very, very tempting.

And yet, not everything is for everyone. If I truly wanted a baby, I would've had one, and these days, it looks like this probably will not happen for me.

That's how I feel today, anyway.

But back in this time period, the question of whether I'd one day become a parent was a much more open question. Things between Sam and I were going relatively well, and we talked a lot about getting married and having kids. But that was In the Future. More important to me at that moment was the secure underpinning of my life—the family of choice I'd purposefully, carefully built around myself, which insulated my ever-more-fragile mental health.

Simply put: my friends were my family, and my family was my life.

I've only ever wanted four or five friends. In theory, I'd love to be one of those people who can send a group text and then have 20 people meet up for drinks, but I'm not. I get stressed out when there's more than six people in a room with me, and I hate large-group brunches—the splitting of the bill alone sends me into paroxysms of anxiety. I want good people I can count on one hand, and I want to see them all the time.

In the spring of 2018, I had just that. Carrie and I would talk about how much we loved living together and how, even though she was planning to leave for law school, she would come back here every summer. She and I came out with this extremely stupid but entertaining joke scheme that made us, and us alone, laugh until we cried.

"So . . . which do you think came first, birdsong or music? Did they inspire us? Or did we inspire them?"

"Handles—did we evolve hands to use them? Or was it the other way around?"

She was just so *funny*. And brilliant. We made plans to

collaborate on a podcast together, called *This Town Is Changing*, about how our little town was lurching forward and backward, simultaneously.

Brooke and I would talk for hours and hours and hours about the most important kind of nothing. We would start talking about, say, a really good dumpling that Brooke had recently, which would lead to a discussion of how *furious* we both are that there aren't any Dunkin' Donuts in Oregon, because of course it's not actually about the doughnuts but the coffee, which then would shoot off into breaking down our 14 favorite things about Eleanor, then quickly segue to Brooke's tales of being an honorary dirtbag townie in Boston. This was maybe the first six minutes of a two-hour dialogue.

With Emily, I knew I could truly tell her anything, that she would never judge but instead just be present. Nothing would shock her, and nothing would make her think I'm a bad person, or unworthy of love. Her empathy and love were like the ocean and felt so unconditional. When we'd talk, she'd gently bring up new perspectives that I would never in a million years have thought of. She taught me patience and kindness by example every day.

I thought, even if Sam and I broke up, I would be lucky to have these brilliant, loving women around me. They were still big parts of my life, certainly in part by virtue of *their* childlessness. Our stability and cohesiveness was a taste of what, perhaps, a true chosen family would give me. Would it make me like Caroline from *Real Housewives* at last, so certain of where, and who, I was?

These women—Carrie, Emily, and Brooke—were my people. They were never going to leave me. And whatever storms raged around me, I was secure in that.

✄

There was another concern racing through my mind as I considered the "kid question"—one that kept me up at night: Would a child with my genes have my wild 'n' wacky brain, too? After all, this depression stuff is genetic; in fact, some scientists now think that five mental health disorders "long thought to be distinct"—autism, ADHD, depression, bipolar disorder, and schizophrenia—may all share a genetic similarity. I can point to the people, on both sides of my family, who have struggled similarly. Did I really want to carry on that tortured legacy into another generation?

In the spring of 2018, my brain truly outdid itself, and I found myself more depressed than ever.

So I tried, very hard, to find any kind of decent mental health care in my town. I had good insurance, an open schedule, and no internal conflict over therapy—and yet it was still fucking impossible. My privileged ass could barely make it happen. Think about the hurdles that Americans who don't have these advantages face every day when they're trying to access help! In the years that have followed, I've thought about it all the damn time, especially as we've all sunk deeper and deeper over the past few years.*

The first big difficulty I faced was actually finding a doctor and getting on the right medication, since mine had stopped working. When I started realizing I needed real help, I found that not a single psychiatrist in my town was accepting new patients. Of course, it took months and months to figure this out. I'd actually

---

*This is exactly why we need Medicare for All. This is an insane system designed to deny people care for profit, and even when you have every resource and great support, it's impossible. It's one of the cruelest things we as a country do.

never been to a psychiatrist—I'd had primary care doctors put me on antidepressants, or mental health nurse practitioners give me therapy and meds but never a legit, gone-to-med-school, specializes-in-medication type.

And of course, navigating the byzantine health care system is impossible, even as a nondepressed person. Just scheduling doctor's appointments is such a goddamn slog. I keep "Call Dr. So-and-So" on my to-do list for weeks or months, and . . . I just don't do it. I don't know why! It's so simple and will take no more than five minutes of my time. I'll call them, find out that no one can see me for eight weeks, put it in my calendar, and go back to my life.

But I don't. I never, ever do. Even when I'm *in the doctor's office after the appointment* and they ask me if I want to schedule the next visit for three months out, I play this dumb game:

"Hmmm, ahhhhhhctually? That month is *pretty* crazy, so I think I'm just going to wait until it gets a little closer to schedule."

That month is *not* crazy for me. That month is exactly like every other month; the only thing I might have on my schedule three months out is a wedding, which almost certainly will not take place at 9:40 a.m. on a Tuesday. I will work at the normal times, see friends at the normal times, and sleep at the normal times. There is no reason for me not to schedule the goddamn thing except some undefinable resistance to . . . what, even?

So that's scheduling a doctor's appointment under ideal circumstances. When you're depressed, finding a psychiatrist who is taking new patients and your insurance is a man on the fucking moon. But Sam had begged me, pleaded with me, to talk to someone, and he wasn't the only one. Brooke, too, had asked what I needed to be able to do this. When two of your closest people seem that afraid for you, it becomes easier to just do the damn thing.

So I tried. Hard. Eventually, I called every psychiatrist in my mid-sized city. I'd go on *Psychology Today*'s website, filter the doctors who took my insurance, and call one at random, leaving a message that was both a cry for help and preemptive effort to spike the relationship:

"Hi, um, this is . . . my name is Kelly Williams Brown, and I, I have . . . I think I need to see someone about depression but also maybe ADHD and medication management, too. I've been very depressed for several months now. But I don't know, maybe we can talk on the phone and see if it's a good fit? It said your specialty is ADHD and depression, but I don't know . . . you, or what you do, and I probably should, right? Anyway, my number is . . ."

What I'm going to say may sound hyperbolic, but I know now, firsthand, that it could save your life: if you struggle with ongoing mental health issues and medication is part of your treatment, *you must* make every possible human effort to *see a psychiatrist*. I guess I always thought of psychiatrists as extra-expensive, difficult-to-find therapists, but they're not. For the most part, you're not there to talk about bad relationship patterns or your mother. You're there because they specialize in brain chemistry; they are uniquely qualified to administer and monitor profoundly powerful medications that, to this day, we as humans do not fully understand.

Despite receiving my first mental health diagnosis as a child and beginning to take brain-altering medication at age nine, I had never in my life seen an actual psychiatrist. That is the equivalent of having had a heart condition since I was young but never once seeing a cardiologist.

Psychiatrists are hard to find, which is just one bit of the 5,000-piece puzzle that is our nation's failure to address mental illness. You will call, and they will not be able to see you for four months. Fine. Get it on the calendar and then ask a friend or a parent or whoever to also put it on *their* calendar and help you get there.

Four months is a ridiculously long time to wait, and it's not fair and also very stupid. But you have to do it anyway because then you will have *established care*. Someone who has seen you before will normally not make you wait months again; they will nearly always be able to get you in much faster. If something is going wrong, you can call them and they will get back to you. With any luck, you can stay with them for years and years. They will know you, and your history, what works, and what could cause cata-strophic harm.

But I didn't know that, so I didn't do it. To me, four months may as well have been four years. I finally found someone—not a psychiatrist but a very nice mental health nurse practitioner who was just getting started in his new career. He was able to prescribe medication, and we talk through my options. Paxil made me kind of crazy when I was a teenager. I loved Wellbutrin, but that's maybe what gave me a seizure in 2012. Zoloft was good until it stopped working. Well, he says, there is something relatively new to the market, and maybe I should try that.

Great, I say, and less than 24 hours later I had a bottle of pills and pages and pages of warnings that I did not read—but who does? Which is why you *really* need to be able to trust the person who gives it to you.

As those pages of warnings were trying to tell me, psychiatric meds are nothing to trifle with and can indeed have deadly conse-quences. Both "mania" and "suicidal ideation" have been listed as side effects on every antidepressant I've ever taken, and yet it had never once crossed my mind that I might experience either.

POSSIBLE SIDE EFFECTS

If I actually stop to think about it, which I don't do for obvious reasons, medication is legitimately terrifying.

Here is this itty-bitty, tiny little chalky thing, 1/300th of the mass of my breakfast, that will kill the strep or make me go to sleep or allow me to feel emotions and get out of bed again. Of *course* it's going to be dangerous. How else could something so small be so powerful?

So, in this, like in so much, I will suspend my disbelief. None of those things will happen to me. I will feel so much better than I do now. Down the hatch.

✄

Say what you will about a mixed manic-depressive state brought on by the wrong antidepressant: it may end at the psychiatric hospital, but it's a creatively fertile time!

Have you ever been in a car—perhaps, dare I say, a zippy li'l Miata—that has tremendous pickup? When you mash your foot down on that pedal, you feel the acceleration in your gut, and it even makes you a tiny bit nauseated, but it's *so* thrilling. That is precisely what happened to my brain.

All of a sudden, I'd left my torpor and was going a million miles an hour. I had so, so, so, *so* many ideas! And I wanted to talk about alllll of them! In fact, I wanted to talk to *everyone* about *everything*. I wanted to let them know how very, very bad things were but, surprise! Now they are so much better. *So* better. This is my *year*!

I tell everyone this. Maybe I was really convincing in my enthusiasm, or maybe no one was able to express to me that they thought something very wrong and pulled away instead. Honestly, I wouldn't have blamed them—by this point, I had been tremendously exhausting for a year and a half.

So there I was, full of ideas and energy and yet, somehow, still depressed. Darkness and hopelessness still percolated in me, but I had a lot of energy! And plans! And impulsivity! This is what's known as a mixed state, and it's super dangerous.

Below, listed from good to not to very, very bad, are just a few of the more groundbreaking ideas I undertook, tried to ensnare others in, and even pitched to my literary agent on the off chance she had serious clout in Apple's industrial design. What a time!

- **A nonprofit women and non-binary coworking/art space:** This would be a cooperative model where there would be everything from full coworking memberships (24-hour access, a physical mailing address, and a desk) to $25 memberships for young people. It was to be in one of these old houses in

my town that are zoned for commercial use and can be rented
for, like, $2,500 a month. The basement would be full of
power tools; a former shop and art teacher would run
seminars, as would anyone who felt comfortable teaching that
kind of stuff. The ground floor would be a social area and
art-making space that the renovation-minded could design,
paint, and remodel. We would have lots of nooks that we
built, because everyone loves working or sitting or reading in
a nook. There would be a kitchen with wine in the fridge. The
top floor would be quiet coworking space with heavy old
wood tables and banker's lamps. We would get together and
have creative brainstorm sessions. Maybe sometimes there
would be shows in the basement. We would call it the Salem
Women's Auxiliary Place. **Objective grade: A.** I still want to
do this, and think it could work, and I have an entire
notebook full of pretty 1910s-style monograms to use as logos.

- **Designing, prepping, and laying a 10 × 8-foot patio:**
  Lugging paving stones around for an afternoon was pretty
  good for my mental state because by the end I was very tired
  and actually able to sleep. Also, I got to spend two days
  filling another notebook with every possible stone pattern,
  so that was fun. All told, this was a reasonably attractive
  addition to my home. **Objective grade: B+.**

- **A little light on your cell phone or work monitor that would
  broadcast your internal state:** The simplest version here
  would be if you're in an antisocial mood, it would glow red,
  whereas if you're feeling chatty and want to engage but are
  just reading something for now and could totally be

interrupted, it's green. I really went deep on this—maybe if you want everyone to know you're doing something serious, like reading a dense novel, it shines a deep federal blue. Maybe if you are being accosted by someone you did not want to talk to, it would strobe red and blue like a tiny ambulance. People around you would see it and come to your rescue. If you were mourning or heartbroken, it would just be a sad bruise color that slowly morphed from transparent purplish to a muted olive. Later, I'd suggest something along this line during the unit meeting at the psych ward. What if we could wear buttons—red, yellow, or green—that would tell other people how we were feeling in that moment, if we didn't feel comfortable communicating our state? The staff seemed really into this idea, going so far as to brainstorm on how we could do that without using pins, which are forbidden. **Objective grade: B-.** This is something that works a lot better as a conceit a precocious child would have in a novel about 9/11 than an actual idea. This doesn't mean it's a *bad* idea.

• **Redecorating my bathroom. Theme: TOUCANS, TOUCANS, TOUCANSSSS!!!** Before I started, my bathroom had modern, stainless-steel finishes and cool gray walls. Now, it's a flamingo pink, with big prints of toucans and gold metal. The centerpiece is this over-the-top shower curtain I sewed myself. The very busy print has toucan couples shyly peeking out from behind banana leaves, and sexy, gendered tigers stalking sexily through bamboo. I did not do the best paint job, and I've only replaced half my stainless-steel fixtures (faucets, showerheads, etc.) with gold ones. **Objective grade: C.** Execution is not great, and no real estate agent would let me put this house on the market without toning it way, way down. But I enjoy it.

• **Renovating my upstairs bathroom, by myself, without any experience:** Demonstrating the never-say-die confidence displayed by the truly incompetent, I have decided to tear out the wood siding, retile the floor, and maybe put up some wallpaper. Hmmm, I can't wallpaper, so I'll paint it jungle green! I hate this sink, so I'll tear it out and install a new one! But I can't install the new one! No sink, yet I am undaunted. Let's replace that light fixture with one I found at the salvage store! Those tiles are almost even! I'll fix that hole and finish painting *at some point!* (I haven't.) **Objective grade: D.** It's reversible but not without some real effort.

• **Carl the Awning:** Here we get into the true *madness.* My back porch isn't covered, and I want it to be! First, I'm gonna give my home address to several awning companies so they'll send me sample fabrics and then catalogs—so many catalogs. I acknowledge, even in this state, that I am not going to spend $7,000 on an awning . . . but what if I made my own?!? Not out of canvas. Don't be silly. I'm going to make it out of six-foot-wide chicken wire! That I will weave ribbons

CARL, THE CHICKEN WIRE AWNING

through in a hexagonal pattern! Then, I'll use my heat gun to carefully melt a clear vinyl shower curtain over it! Then I'll attach it to the cedar tree and to my house, method TBD! **Objective grade: F.** And I wish at least one of the many people I talked to about this would've gotten in touch with my mom. A six-foot bundle of chicken wire with a bunch of ribbons woven through, proudly exhibited by someone with long, thin cuts all over her hands talking very fast should trigger at least a little concern. I totally get why they didn't. But I wish they had. I was not myself. I was out of my mind.

I truly wonder, sometimes, why no one said anything. But perhaps they did, and I didn't, or couldn't, listen.

No one in my little chosen family was doing great. My energy, my intensity was starting to wear thin on my friends.

And more to the point, they were facing their own shit. Everyone had been depressed anyway, but that spring it felt like things were veering out of control. Brooke had decamped for an exciting new job in Portland, which meant the most consistent person in my orbit was gone. Carrie and Emily were struggling: long-term boyfriends had been broken up with, huge future decisions were being made, and, to be frank, while I was doing the worst, no one seemed especially seaworthy.

To top it all off, Sam and I were fighting more and more. There was a lot of drinking, a lot of feelings, and a lot of yelling. Nights often ended in tears.

Finally, I decided I could not take it and could no longer be with Sam. A few hours after I broke up with him, my father called to confirm his cancer diagnosis.

After I hung up the phone, I text Carrie and Emily. I wait for a reply. Nothing.

An hour goes by. One texts back about feeling overwhelmed, and the other says she needs a little bit of space. For the first time in almost a decade, my chosen family isn't there. They are avoiding me, and I don't know why.

I'm flabbergasted as this reality begins to cement over the next few days. I am so, so confused, and no one will give me an answer. I begin to flail and truly freak out. Earlier in the winter, they'd both gone to Mexico for a week and a half, and I'd felt so bereft and adrift. I remember being afraid that maybe their plane would crash on the way home, and I'd be exactly this lonely forever. And now, two months later, that nightmare had come true. They were just . . . gone, and the more I reached out trying to figure out what was going on, the more they pulled away.

There is, as you can imagine, a lot of backstory here, and much of it is exceptionally personal. I will say, with the benefit of hindsight, that I definitely said and did many things that contributed. I'd been exhausting for a year and then all of a sudden not only was I depressed, I was manic, *and* I was breaking up with my boyfriend, *and* my dad had cancer, and I was just such an emotional black hole. There was also some stuff that truly wasn't about me and isn't my story to tell.

Maybe part of it was that I'd always been the mother of the group, and probably at times an overbearing one. I was the one with the space to crash in and cash if you needed it, and I was the one who, when you said you had a stomachache, started asking you questions and then drove you to the hospital for your appendectomy. But I had ceased to uphold my part of the bargain. And now I needed them—still, again, more—and they were gone.

I'd no more thought these friendships could go away than I thought my parents or sisters could divorce me. If you'd asked me what the worst thing was that could happen to me, short of a family member dying, it would be this.

I went from having three people—Carrie, Sam, and Emily— always around me to having no one in town I felt close enough to talk about this with. After a few weeks, I'm ashamed to say, I got back together with Sam. I needed him. I needed to not be alone. I needed someone to choose me. And for a little while, at least, it worked. But then I got to my very, very worst mixed-state idea:

- **Killing myself on a whim:** It's been a bad year! A worse month! An unbearable night! I am tired of feeling this way, I have felt this way for so long, and I have tried so hard not to feel this way. But here I am! What if I didn't feel anything, didn't have to confront the utter shitshow my life had become in the past 16 months? I have a ton of can-do attitude and *no* impulse control! I am manic *and* depressed! I am full of innovative ideas; I am thinking *outside* the box! I could do it *right now! Nothing* could be worse than this! **Objective grade: 0, none out of 100, absolutely no points awarded.** This was my worst-ever thought, which led to my worst-ever action, and hands-down the most destructive and awful thing I have ever, ever done.

✄

Bad Decisions Charm Bracelet

Decide on a theme. Your own Bad Decisions will be represented by different charms than mine. I've included doodles for my charms below, but feel free to personalize this to your own liking and situation. Life is a rich tapestry!

Materials:

- A pencil
- Regular printer paper, or any paper, doesn't matter
- An oven
- Masking tape (optional; for those who cannot trust themselves to trace something unsecured carefully)
- A pack of Shrinky Dinks paper—glossy or matte, your choice. I like matte. You can also do this with No. 6 plastic containers (the clear, bubble-like clamshell food containers often used for a salad or whatever)
- Colored pencils or colored Sharpies (You can use regular markers I guess, but it's going to be super smudgy. Make sure whichever you choose, you have a black one that is thin for outlining.)
- Scissors

- Hole punch
- Something flat you can bake something on (Probably a cookie sheet, but I've used Pyrex casserole pans and everything turned out just fine.)
- Something to line said baking item, like aluminum foil or parchment paper (Honestly, I've baked things right on the Pyrex or whatever, but I'm sure I'm exposing myself to chemicals that will perhaps cause a Shrinky Dink–related cancer down the line,* so I cannot in good conscience tell you to do the same. But your charms would be fine if you did.)
- A chain that is the right length for your (or whomever's) wrist
- Jump rings
- Needle-nose pliers or fingernails you don't care about
- A clasp

---

*I do not have a single scrap of evidence for this except my firmly held belief that everything causes cancer . . . so I may as well go ahead and smoke.

Instructions:

1. Using a normal pencil, draw your own charms on a piece of paper. You can also print out images from online and trace those. You want fairly simple images here. Remember that it's going to become a third of the size it is now—so a 3-inch (7.6cm) drawing will be a 1-inch (2.5cm) charm.

2. Draw, I don't know, nine things? Seven things? If you draw an odd number of things, it's going to be easier to space them out on your chain. Draw as many as you want.

3. Preheat the oven to 325 degrees Fahrenheit (162 degrees Celsius).

4. Tape your paper to a surface. Set your Shrinky Dink paper down on top of it, rough side up. Tape that down, too.

5. Use either a black colored pencil or a black, thin Sharpie to trace the charms onto the Shrinky Dink paper.

6. Color in the charms. Colored pencils work, but if you use Sharpies, honestly, it's easier and the colors will be very bold. Either way, coloration will be amplified.

7. Carefully cut out your charms. Remember to leave space at the top of the Shrinky Dink paper to punch a hole so you can affix it to the bracelet.

8. Punch a hole through each charm.

9. Set your charms on your lined baking sheet, rough side up.

10. Put them in the oven.

11. Sit in front of the oven and watch them. This is only going to take a couple minutes. At first, they will shrink. Then they will puff upward or curl, and you will think, *Ah, these are so small! They* must *be done!* They are not done. Quiet the part of you that says they are.

12. When they flatten back out, wait another 30 seconds.

13. Take them out!

14. Wait a few minutes and then get them off their sheet or out of their pan. They'll need to cool for a few minutes—just set them on a plate.

15. Decide on your charm order. Figure out where the middle of the chain is; that is where your middle charm will go. Use a jump ring to attach it. To open the jump ring (if it isn't already), slide it onto your needle-nose pliers and open them slightly. Put the jump ring through the hole in the charm and the bracelet, and use the pliers to squish it closed.

16. Figure out where all the other charms are going to go. You can eyeball this or, if you want to be really precise, you can count links. This is where having an odd number of charms comes in handy: if you have seven, you just have to gauge halfway between the middle charm and the ends and then halfway between that.

17. Attach the charms in the correct places.

18. Attach the clasp parts.

19. *Charm bracelet!*

✂

Something to Do When You Are About to Make a Bad Decision

I'm going to lay all my cards on the table, here: as you have probably gathered from the contents of this book, I do not always make the best decisions. But I've found something that at least helps, which is building in mental speed bumps to at least slow down, if not stop, the process.

1. Admit to yourself that you might be about to make a bad decision. Tell yourself that if you do, it's not great, but it's probably not the end of the world. Do *not* get into self-loathing at this stage because then you'll impulsively do something to quiet that line of thought. Just think, *Huh, I really want to do XYZ, and I know I probably shouldn't.*

2. Decide to wait for 10 minutes. Set your phone timer! Just give it a 10-minute pause before you text him or order that next drink or bum a cigarette after you haven't had one in months or order Postmates even though you have no money.

3. Tell yourself that if, in 10 minutes, you still want this thing, you can have it.

4. Wait, wait, wait, wait.

5. If you notice, during this period, your brain screaming at you to do XYZ, think, *Yep, that's kind of what my mind does during these times.* You only have to make it seven more minutes, so be calm.

6. You may well be using this time for justification! It makes *sense* to do this . . . because you want to. This is a nice time to ask yourself if there is something *else* you can do. Can you text this message to a friend? Get a Diet Coke? Stand up and leave this area where people are smoking? Walk over to your fridge and see what's in there?

7. After 10 minutes, reassess.

8. Repeat, forever, for the rest of your life.

CHAPTER 7

My Almost-Dying

In Which I Do the Worst Thing

ALL RIGHT, SO HERE'S THE DARKEST BIT OF THE BOOK. IT revolves around the saddest, most awful thing I have ever done, so there's nothing I can say that makes this not, y'know, *kind of a bummer.* If reading about suicide stuff and hospitalization bothers you, you should skip the next two chapters.

✂

A SELECTION of INACCURATE THOUGHTS·

"No one would miss you."

"Eleanor will be fine."

"It's never going to get better."

"You will never have friends this close again."

"Everyone is talking about you."

"This is all YOUR FAULT."

"If anyone cared, they'd be here.*"

* They actually were.

The only thing that saved me was some incredible luck. Or, more accurately, the only thing that saved me was Sam.

I came up with a plan to kill myself and put it into action in a matter of minutes, in the middle of the night, while Sam lay asleep upstairs, oblivious. And by some extremely lucky fluke, he woke up and found me. He doesn't know why he woke up. Later, at the hospital, the doctor told me I would've been dead within the next three to five minutes if Sam hadn't found me.

This, more than perhaps anything else, is what haunts him. He tells me in a shaky voice days, weeks, months later—*he so, so easily could have not woken up.* I should've died; the doctor was surprised I did not. It was, as they put it in the ER while trying to find an open psychiatric hospital bed for me, a "high-lethality attempt."

If it had been another organ experiencing catastrophic failure, it would be an unfortunate but understandable tale. If I were rushed to the hospital very, very sick, stayed there for three days, saw a competent specialist, and left knowing how to take care of myself and with a good care team, that would be a very good story!

I could've told people and asked if they would come see me. My mom could've told her friends. Maybe they would've even offered to bring over a casserole. In the future, when I was feeling whole, I could feel resilient and grateful. It would be proof that I'm strong rather than proof that I'm damaged. But it wasn't that, not quite.

When it's your brain that goes haywire for one brief, horrible moment, the overriding emotion that lingers in the aftermath is simply shame.

My suicide attempt surprised everyone, including me. If you'd asked me that day, "Are you suicidal?" I would've said no and been slightly shocked. But if you asked me, "Have you spent months idly pondering how someone—not *you*, of course, just some hypothetical human—could quickly and certainly kill themselves using things around this house?" Well. That's a different question, isn't it? As my friend Henrietta put it, "It would've been that fucking *stupid* thing of, 'Oh noooooo, a beautiful girl killed herself, and *no one knows why!*'"

I know why. I believe, and my psychiatrist has subsequently affirmed, that the new medication prescribed to me a few months prior to my suicide attempt just wasn't working right with my brain. As a result, I was in a uniquely fragile and dangerous place mentally. Essentially, I was still depressed, but I now had many of the symptoms of mania—like excessive talking, grandiose ideas, and risky behaviors. So I was still sad, but now my darkest thoughts weren't hindered by lethargy and ennui but rather could be acted upon with the same gusto and impetuousness I'd brought to the rest of my life since starting this new medication a few months prior. On that night, there were maybe 10 minutes between my decision to take my life and the action I undertook to do it.

My mental state was exacerbated by a bunch of factors. My dad had cancer. By now, Sam and I had completely broken down as a couple. But mainly, the inciting incident was what the hospital later described as "catastrophic loss of chosen family."

When the breakdown between my friends and I happened, I knew everyone would choose Carrie because she is preferable. I didn't blame them. As I said earlier, I hadn't been much of a friend or a person for years, and they've all known her much longer.

But it hurt—so much—to know that I was not being chosen. It hurt even more to be alone in my house, to have no one to cook for, no one to watch *CBS Sunday Morning* with, no one to buy a leather purse with a Collie painted on it for.

Someone on Reddit once said that when you break up with someone, you lose the language you've cultivated just between yourselves. My language with them—weird inside jokes, shared opinions and politics, snarky observations of just about everyone who lives in our town, every memory, all of it—was gone, and the vacuum it left was unfathomable.

As with any breakup, it wasn't just the present that was painful. It was all the memories of the past—at beach houses together, having our Christmas party, fucking around and doing nothing in the backyard. Were all these memories still valid? Could I still cherish them? It also obliterated any future in which these women were always present in my life, something I'd taken for granted until it was untrue.

I felt like I'd lost a layer of skin but couldn't tell anyone. What do you even say as a mid-30s woman? Help, I'm sad. My friends don't like me. The people in my life who I chose just unchose me?

Not that I would've talked to anyone, really. I live in a small town, and our estrangement didn't go unnoticed. I felt like everyone was watching me, that maybe they knew things about me I did not want them to know. I was so ashamed of the circumstances. It felt like the time in sixth grade when I was the new girl. At first, the popular girls found me to be an interesting novelty—did I often see those skulls with the horns in Texas? But eventually they decided they did *not* like me, which they all circled up to tell me one day on the playground. After they were done explaining why I was no longer friends with any of them, they started sprinting up with people who were good candidates for me to be friends with now—mostly fourth-grade boys and the two outcasts in the grade whose ranks I have now clearly joined.

Twenty years later, the feelings of abandonment I felt were

familiar, and I was in awful shape. Before the attempt, I was crying day and night. I couldn't remember a single time in my adult life when I'd felt so alone. My house, so recently filled with people I love, was now entirely empty, and I blamed myself. It felt like no one was coming to help me, and even if they were, I didn't know what could help me. I'd tried so hard, and yet for 18 months, life had just been one horrible surprise after another, each timed to hit just as I thought I might finally be getting back on my feet.

Now, there is nothing. My friends are gone. Sam and I reach a new level of dysfunction. I am afraid to be out in public; I perceive people acting distantly toward me and wonder who has heard what. My dad has a hole in his stomach that he has to eat through. My cat is dead, and I cannot save my grandmother from the life she lived. I had a husband, but I left him—I left everyone. A crazy man is the president, and kids live in cages.

Things that were objectively in the past begin swirling around and around until they feel like the present: the Gorge is on fire, and the car is covered with dead-baby-deer ash. Buffalo Bayou keeps rising until it sloshes into my second-grade bedroom. I'm in the tub, and I'm crying in frustration because I have no arms and have been trying for 10 minutes to figure out how I can get out. At the hospital, the physician's assistant ignores me as I beg, snot dripping down my face, for help, and the security guard sneers at me. Ohio, Michigan—it's his horrible face on every TV in the bar, I want to get down on the ground under the keno machine, I want to save myself, but all of this is so much bigger than me, and I can't fight anymore.

So in the tick-tock of that night, I make and act upon an awful decision. Time I am not present for passes. Sam wakes up, finds me, rescues me, and I wake up on the bathroom floor. "We have to go to the hospital," he tells me, and even though I do not agree with him, we are soon in the car, heading to the small-town hospital where everyone had always told me to go rather than the one that discharged me with the dislocated shoulder. It's a clear night, you can see all the stars, and we are both quiet. What would I even say? Sam is furious; his jaw is in that position, his eyes are slightly bugged, and he will not talk to or even look at me.

One of the nurses recognizes me from my newspaper column days, which earns her the weakest smile any human has produced to date. Everyone around me is cheerful and upbeat, except, of course, for Sam and now my mother, who has appeared after driving down from Portland. She is mainly in problem-solving mode, but every now and again her face seems to crumple when she doesn't think anyone is looking at her. Then she smooths it back out and asks the practical questions.

Periodically, someone comes in the room to try to figure out the extent of the damage I've done to my own body. I cannot remember now if I walked down the hallways, or was in a wheelchair, or was in a bed. Everything has a hazy, dreamlike quality.

"Lots of people, they just take a few aspirin and *say* they want to die, but *you* meant it!" the very kind ER doctor says with something that sounds a tiny bit like begrudging approval. He pushes a few buttons, and I slide into the CT scanner to see how much of my brain is dead from oxygen deprivation. He doesn't call me "missy," but it's implied, and I'm grateful for his attitude toward all of this. He is acting as though I did something incredibly stupid but also kind of hilarious, and now I'm tangled up in a fence or something.

A nurse comes in with an adorable but confusing thing. It is, upon examination, an upside-down American-flag-themed frozen yogurt container with a little American-flag toothpick, plus red, white, and blue tinsel glued around the edges and a carefully cut-out sign that says:

Thinking of you,
FROM SILVERTON MIDDLE SCHOOL 2

It is hideous. It is wonderful. It is grotesquely inappropriate and yet perfect for the current moment.

I look at her, confused.

"Broughtcha something!" she says, beaming. "So today is actually Memorial Day, and the kids always make these for veterans in the hospital."

"Huh!" I say. I am not a veteran.

"And on other holidays, too! But this one is for veterans."

I stare at her, saying nothing. As a crafter, I have to appreciate the sheer effort in this janky little yogurt-cup trophy, if not the execution (which is a bit haphazard for even my low standards).

"We had extra, and I thought you might enjoy one."

My mother, who, like me, has always adored a small town and a ticky-tacky craft, is instantly taken by this weird little art.

"Awwwwww, that's so *cute*! And *nice*! I wish *my* students would do something like that!"

In this moment, I am struck by how different this hospital visit is from the one where they discharged me with the dislocated and broken shoulder. So I will say this again, as everyone had always said it to me: *If you are in Salem and you get injured, go to Silverton Hospital.* The 30-minute drive is worth it! I managed a crooked, broken smile as I looked at the nurse.

"Thank you," I said. And I meant it.

Today, this installation lives in the little glass cabinet that has my altar on top, and I love that the tiny beacon of hope on my darkest night was, in fact, a craft. I so, so wish I could thank the artist.

✄

Now it's been 10 hours, and I'm just lying on the bed waiting, although for what I'm not sure. The wonderful social worker comes in and says he doesn't know about *me*, but *he* sure thinks I should go get some inpatient treatment. As in, going to a psych ward. He can't actually make me go—the whole involuntary admission thing is way more complicated than you'd think—but he'll bet my mom and boyfriend would feel a *lot better if I did!*

I do not want to go. At all. My logic: the psychiatric hospital is for people who are really sick. I, meanwhile, am *perfectly fine.* I made a bad decision that didn't work out, and now I'd love to pretend nothing happened. I lay out these arguments and push back against everything he's saying.

But then I look at Sam and my mom. Sam looks absolutely haunted, and I begin to realize the horror of the scene he walked in on, and how he must have felt as he rushed to save my life. Later, he tells me, it hit him on the drive back to the hospital, when he brought my stuff. It all landed on him in the car, and he was howling. I do not know it yet, but this—specifically, finding me near death—had deeply traumatized him, and he would later seek treatment for PTSD. I had done something to him that could not be undone.

And then there is my mom. My mom is the steadiest. She's so warm, but she's also a very practical, get-it-done person in moments of crisis. And yet she, too, looks shattered and terrified. As far as she knew, her daughter was having a really hard time, but she was also not a suicidal person. Until she was woken up with a phone call at 2 a.m. and found out she was. I wonder, now, what she was thinking and how she felt as she drove down from Portland across dark country roads, and hope I never find out.

They both look more tired and sad than any humans have ever looked, and the last thing I want to do right now is make them sadder and more tired, so yes, fine: I'll go. Can I go tomorrow? Can I go home first and pack? Can I drive myself?

I can*not* do *any* of that, no, the social worker tells me, and then heads out to continue working the phones on my behalf. He comes in periodically to update us: there are no beds anywhere in the state. He's called Portland, Eugene, and Bend but not found anything. Then I guess someone tells him what I did, and he comes back a few hours later looking triumphant.

"So be*cause* this was high-lethality, we've managed to jump the line, and they've got a bed for you!" he says, and I so wish I had it in me to be like, "OMG, *James,* yaaaaay!"

I'm going to the newly opened top-of-the-line psychiatric hospital in Portland—Unity, it's called, because it's the joint effort of four regional hospitals—so now we're just waiting for the secure medical transport to come. Sam has brought me a suitcase full of clothes he packed and cozy socks he bought me at Rite Aid that say "SUNDAY BRUNCH DAY." This suitcase *also* contains a very personal item that I'd brought on my last trip and apparently never unpacked, although I will not know this until I am discharged and it is handed to me along with other forbidden items in a clear plastic bag.

Now I am walking out to the parking lot, and now I am in the full-size American sedan with bars across the windows wondering how long to wait before I ask them if we can smoke.

There are several placards in the back seat warning that, if I misbehave, I might be put in restraints. They remind me sternly that I *cannot* be kicking the back of the front seats, or screaming, or lighting cigarettes. I cannot open the doors or roll down the windows, which are barred; areas where one might try to slam their head are padded. I gaze out the window at red barns and rolling fields and think about how life contains all sorts of surprises.

A man who looks like Craig Robinson is driving, along with a sturdy woman who looks like a composite of the first 10 Google Image search results for "Montana bartender." They're so pleasant and calm. It's nice to meet me, they say. Been a *pretty big night*, huh? Well, that's okay! It's actually a really nice drive between Silverton and Portland. They've done this drive before; it's a nice one. I look out the window at a strip mall I once parked in to go to a wine-tasting at the Oregon Garden and wonder how I came to occupy these circumstances. In the past 12 hours, I have just become a woman who tried to kill herself, and very nearly did, and now cannot be trusted to transport myself, and I'm not sure I like this new version of me.

I shoot my shot on having a cigarette—I haven't had one since arriving in the hospital 14 hours earlier, could we stop for a smoke?—and, to my astonishment, indeed we can. We pull over in the parking lot of the Silverton Safeway, and the three of us each light one. I'm not disappointed that I lived—honestly, pretty neutral on that one—but I *am* disappointed that I now have to deal with the consequences of my actions. I want, so bad, to sprint away from them and this whole rigmarole, which, with each moment, is becoming a bigger and bigger pain in the ass.

But I don't run away. I sit on the curb and start asking them questions about their work because their job is *wild* and what else am I up to? I find out that the longest drive they've been on was to Colorado, ferrying a mentally imbalanced teenager, although they also transport perfectly balanced teenagers in custody situations, which is so dark. Sometimes they do regular medical transport, in which case the protocol is different, but mostly it's secure. On some level, I guess it's kind of cool that I'm now an asset to be guarded.

The guy tells me what he says he tells everyone he transports in my current circumstances: He hopes that I take this as an opportunity to rest, to reset, to try again. That it is never too late for anyone, and if I'm still here, there's a reason. He guesses everyone needs a break every now and again. I should take the break and make the most of it. I should take it and use it to figure out what it is I'm still here to do.

✂

A reminder of all this lives, to this day, in my house. When I first got home from the hospital, there was a little trail of blood droplets on the hardwood floor leading from the bathroom to the kitchen. I sprayed them with Mrs. Meyer's Clean Day spray and then scrubbed them away . . . except for one the size of a pencil eraser in the hallway. For reasons that I didn't and don't understand, I left it. It is still there.

Every now and again when I'm mopping, I'll see it and think, *Oh, that. There it is. Should I mop it? I should mop it. This is weird, and insanely morbid. Most people certainly do not leave two-year-old blood on their floor. Why is this on my floor? I should mop it.*

Then I don't.

This dark little blotch, every now and again, forces me to face the goddamn thing. I am separated from that version of me by years and tremendous effort, but I was right there in the little hallway, and always will have been, bleeding from the nose and mouth as Sam tore the house apart looking for the kitchen shears to cut me out of the mess I had gotten myself in.

~THE TELLTALE~

YEP... I'M STILL HERE.

HARDWOOD SPLOTCH

CHAPTER 8

Psych Ward Crafting

In Which I Lose All My Freedoms but Gain Some New Makeup Skills

THINGS YOU CANNOT HAVE IN A PSYCHIATRIC **ward:** anything metal; anything of length—flexible string, cord, etc.—longer than four inches; items that can conceal other items; the ability to pee without a nurse nearby; access to the craft room for more than 45 minutes per day (on account of very dangerous, forbidden yarn); a sense that you are a real human being with agency, goals, emotions, and actions instead of a sulky cloud that drifts aimlessly from movement therapy to SKIP-BO games to arguing with a mean lady who says I am an evil omen while we watch the communal TV; and a goddamn cigarette.

Things you can have in a psychiatric ward: the kind of ice they give you at Sonic that is super good for crunching;* 22-ounce hot/cold Solo cups that are perfect; Bluetooth headphones; *lots* of

---

* It's called pellet or nugget ice! And in the late 2010s, an "affordable" home pellet ice maker was made that's *only* $500. Someday, it will be mine.—A girl who regularly posts on the icechewing.com message boards

FORBIDDEN:

PHONE CHARGER: NO!

EARBUDS: LOL, NO.

YARN: ARE YOU **FUCKING KIDDING?!**

PENS: ABSOLUTELY <u>NOT</u>.

ALLOWED:

CRUNCHY PELLET ICE!

BAD WI-FI!

MEDS, MEDS, **MEDS!**

VAPORWAVE 22-OZ HOT/COLD SOLO CUP

NICORETTE- DAY & NIGHT!

SKIP-BO!
CARD GAMES I DON'T KNOW!

computer paper if you ask nicely; *coloring books*—my God, the coloring books!; visitors who bring you snacks; a whole bunch of meds; all the nicotine gum you want; slow internet; many half-filled-out workbooks about anger; and every Dean Koontz novel ever.

At the hospital, they have me change out of my clothes and into evergreen scrubs and thick socks with no-slip dots on the bottom. They take an extremely unflattering picture of me; I am not looking my best. I have two black eyes and huge bruises all over, some the size of bread plates. I look like someone beat the shit out of me (sort of true!), or I look like I am dead, and yet here I am, decidedly not. Also, an extremely upset naked man keeps opening the door to the bathroom and screaming; someone is in there to help wash him because of a poo situation.

I want nothing more than to be in a small room with a door I can lock and quietly listen to a soothing podcast and smoke out a window. This is not in the cards.

Although I am at the psychiatric hospital, I am not yet completely admitted. There will be a room for me, they say, probably sometime in the next 24 to 48 hours. But there isn't one now, and so I'm in something of a holding pattern.

In the meantime, I'm led to their very innovative, newfangled Psychiatric Emergency Room. It's a big, open space the size of a high school cafeteria full of comfortable, medical-grade recliners. Sounds relaxing! But it's not because you're in the same barrier-free space with dozens of people who are unwell.

Some are sitting quietly or dozing in their chairs, cocooned in a million hospital blankets so only their heads are poking out. But there are also a whole, whole bunch of people who are yelling, most of whom are men, and all of whom are setting off very loud internal bells.

Logically, I know that this is the safe, good place for them—our society does terribly at helping people with mental illness, and these are the lucky few who are getting help. Nonetheless, I am in a room with many people in active mental breakdowns, people who shortly before now were screaming at strangers on streets. Now I am a stranger they can scream at, and I can't be anywhere but right here with them.

On the upside, there are friendly volunteers, a snack station, coloring books, a phone you can use to make calls, and, most importantly, a sedative (maybe Valium?) staff seemed to be handing out frequently and generously.

"Hiiiiiiiii," a lovely volunteer says, sidling up to me. She has big brown eyes, beautiful and cowlike in the way I envy. "How are you doing? How are you feeling? Talk to me."

"Not, I mean, not *great*, you know?"

She nods gently, understandingly. "What's wrong?"

"Well, there are . . . there's a lot of men here, and they're yelling and seem upset, and I don't know if one of them is going to attack me. And I'm scared right now. And I'm thirsty. And I want a cigarette, and I want some Diet Coke, maybe, iced tea, I don't know. And I don't, you know, I don't *like* this. This is very new for me."

She gazes at me, holding gentle, nonthreatening eye contact. "So . . . I'm not sure we have Diet Coke or iced tea, I'll go check for you. I know we have some cheese and crackers and granola bars and maybe some ice cream—does any of that sound good to you?"

I say that it does and then ask how long I'm going to be in this room.

"I don't really know. I can ask one of the nurses to do a check-in."

I look back at her. She's so thin and tall and looks like a model, but her eyes have seen some shit. And she is here, now, on her own time, not being paid, to see if I need a snack. She feels like such safety.

I go over to the bank of free phones, call my mom, and talk to her for a bit about God knows what. I am so, so grateful for access to my mom. A nurse comes around to tell me that it is still probably going to be another day or so, but she heard that I'm feeling anxious, and how would I feel about taking a sedative?

This is the first thing I've felt sure about in months. I would truly, truly love a sedative, and so she gives me one, and I go into this weird on-and-off sleep. I don't know how much time passes, and I think I remember taking more of whatever it was.

I'm assuming this liberal tranquilizer policy is because everyone who shows up at a psychiatric hospital in crisis could probably benefit from a good 24 hours of sleep, but I'm not a doctor.

Even with the benefit of pills, I am panicked anew every time I wake up. I pull my chair into a corner (less fronts to defend) near some nonthreatening women who have gathered for mutual protection, and doze off. Every few hours someone—a nurse? a doctor? surely not a volunteer—comes around to wake me up and ask me how I'm feeling. I tell them I'm very scared and that I do *not* like this and honestly, I know this likely isn't going to happen, but if *possible*, I'd *love* to step outside and have a cigarette.

That is *absolutely not* going to happen, they tell me, but they are good enough to look legitimately bummed on my behalf.

After about 24—or 36? 48? truly could not tell you—hours, someone gently wakes me up to let me know that a room is ready for me in Three West, and I'm being admitted.

I walk through many, many, many locked doors, the faceless

person booping me through them with their ID. They are such heavy doors, opening with a little click and closing with a heavy thud. At a certain point, I think we are actually making laps, that there is nothing in my future but an endless loop of doors. This will go on for days, until I stumble out a back door and into the sun, blinking and fully cured.

Finally, a door that looks exactly like every other door opens, and I'm looking at a little TV room as a high-definition evangelist calls me to Jesus, which felt a little too on the nose.

And now, I'm here. Just here. The place I will be until I can convince a lot of people otherwise.

The horror of Inpatient isn't *One Flew Over the Cuckoo's Nest.* It's not overstimulation; it's not that people are screaming; it's not cruel nurses or dead-eyed doctors. Honestly, everything is pretty nice in here, and there's a fridge full of snacks—up to and including little orange-and-vanilla ice-cream cups—that I can have anytime.

I guess I assumed it would all be like the psychiatric ER, loud and terrifying and uncertain, and it's not. It's quiet and calm. I have been put in the "easiest" ward, where they do not use restraints, physical or otherwise. That said, all the doors are locked, and I can't leave, and there is *nothing* I hate more than being in a room I can't leave or a situation where someone else has to let me out. My distaste of planes, letting other people drive, and baby showers all spring from this.

And this is just . . . waiting. It is the tick, tick, tick of the large clock over the nurses' station. It is having all the time in the world and not a single thing to do with it.

I have no choices to make, except whether I will attend craft/music/introspection hour (yes); whether I want to spend the rest of the day sitting in my room listening to *Law & Order: Special Victims Unit*, which my roommate is streaming without headphones (no); or whether I will walk back and forth between the farthest locked doors in the unit with my high heels click-click-clicking, making the same powerful sounds they did when I walked on-stage for my book party (yes). If I do 33 back-and-forths, a sign tells me, that's a whole mile! I do 67 clattery laps.

When you have no agency, nowhere to go, and nothing to do, time moves differently. It oozes and seeps by, becoming an oppressive and thick thing. There is absolutely nothing to be done with or in it. It is instead just something you wade slowly through on your way to . . . well, either leaving or dying, I guess.

And I know that I'm not going to be here long, but a lot of people here are. They have stories of prior hospitalizations, of other wards, of being civilly committed by their goddamn traitor families, of waiting to find out if they have to be transferred to the Oregon State Hospital, which—fun fact—*was* the inspiration for *One Flew Over the Cuckoo's Nest*, though it is a very nice, patient-centric place now.

What I truly cannot wrap my mind around is being here forever. Never being able to choose what you want for dinner, or cook it. Never petting your dog, or stepping outside to walk around the block on a nice day. No plans with friends except seeing them sit across a table from you in the Visitor's Room, trying to hide their understandable discomfort. You do not realize how many hundreds of little decisions you make every day until they are all taken away from you, and you find yourself floating in space.

That said: the environment itself is nice! The staff is ridiculously kind and helpful. It's all pastels and framed pictures of the Oregon outdoors and spaces designed to foster socialization

TOILET PAPER IN ITS SAFETY COVE!

and, in my favorite touch and honestly something I'd like to see widely adopted, this satisfying little round hollow in the bathroom where you tuck the toilet paper.

There are so many comfortable, if not comforting, touches. The giant recliners from the Psychiatric ER are here, too, and they're great. You can make them into a bed of sorts, a way comfier bed than my mattress, which seems to be stuffed with plastic bags that crinkle every time I move.

The chair in my room is by a window that looks out on a small, prewar apartment building. On the ground floor is a tiny bistro chair set owned (presumably) by the cute man who comes out periodically to smoke or let his cute corgi go to the bathroom. I watch him sipping beer one evening, and it looks like the wildest freedom. At this point, I've been here for maybe 48 hours. To be fair, though, it would be an awful shame to go to the sanitarium and not spend *any* time gazing at a handsome stranger and creating a fantasy life with him, one in which none of the furniture is upholstered in poo-proof vinyl.

Fellow patients and staff members keep assuming I'm a new therapist because instead of the omnipresent dark green scrubs, I'm wearing long-sleeve dresses and nude heels, and I've picked

MY PRECIOUS

TAKE A 12-HOUR VALIUM NAP!

COMFY!

SAFE!

FRESHLY SANITIZED!

BEST CHAIR EVER

PUSH IT TO SAFETY!

LAYS FLAT!

up on their vocabulary quickly. I am *anxious* in this *milieu*,* but I am also *oriented*** and *in no apparent distress*. I'm also spending a lot of time on my makeup and hair. My occupational therapist asks me why I'm bothering, and I say, "What else am I going to do? My schedule is pretty open."

This is also part of a concerted effort on my part to make everyone think I am just fine, that there was a weird misunderstanding, but things are cool now, and, therefore, I should be discharged ASAP. I had, at that point, years of perfecting my "I'm great!" mask, and this must be my finest performance.

I chat with the staff about normal stuff—the shows we like, trips we've been on or are planning, which Oregon beach is our favorite, how the Blazers might do next year. I do not chat with them about the fact that I have not been functional for years now. Instead, I hype up the bizarre effect the medication had on me, and the unprecedented, destabilizing, ne'er-to-be-repeated loss of my chosen family. I don't mention the scarf-pulling incident from a few months earlier, the one that predated this "official" suicide attempt. I want this all to look like a freakish, once-in-a-lifetime situation that doesn't need to be examined too closely.

This makes my mother, who is correct in her assessment that I am clearly not okay, extremely frustrated. Every time she comes to visit and talk with my providers, they reassure her that this was a one-time thing, that I'm basically fine.***

"I mean, I *hear* you saying she's okay," my mother said to the hospital's psychiatrist. "But, you know, I'm looking at my daughter

---

* General surrounding, including people and activities.

** I know where I am and what's going on.

*** I wasn't!

who tried to kill herself without any warning a few days ago, so I think I'd be a *lot* more comfortable with more evidence."

In retrospect, I probably put on too good of a performance because when I do leave, I am directed to a therapist rather than the more intensive program I need.

✄

Makeup Tips to Make You Look Not Quite as Dead

So you find yourself in a psychiatric ward looking like someone kicked the shit out of you—hey, we've *all* been there! Here are some quick, fun tips you can use as part of a coordinated effort to snow your care team into thinking there's nothing wrong with you in order to be discharged sooner!

• I like to always start with a moisturized face. In this case, I let EltaMD UV Physical sunscreen do double-duty—not only is it a great moisturizing primer, but it also protects me from the sun for the 15 minutes a day I get to be outside.

• Using a green-tinged BB cream will offset some of the redness created by burst blood vessels. Don't forget to finish it with a compatible foundation. This calls for full coverage!

• Undereye concealer, which you will need a lot of to cover two black eyes, should always be slowly and gently patted in with a ring fin-ger, the same way you'd apply an eye cream.

• You may be tempted to go full glam because your life is now just meaningless hours and nothing to fill them with, but resist the urge! Your mirror is essentially a cookie tin, so you are *not* gonna get the results you want. Try a fresh, clean look instead—think soft pink eyeshadow with maybe a little black liquid liner.

✄

I tend to avoid my room because my roomie is in there. She's been here for months, although according to her, she will soon be transferred to the state penitentiary's psychiatric facility. Her ex-husband, she tells me, is the one who lied and put her here. The story is horrific, but (and?) she does not seem super well.

She's clearly used to having a new roommate every few days—mine seems to be the designated "Depressed Girl Who Tried and Failed to Kill Herself" bed. It feels like she has seen dozens of me come and go. She asked if I've ever been to a psychiatric hospital before, and when I say no, she said, "Huh. Well, you got a lot to learn," but doesn't elaborate.

This room is hers. And in this room, *Law & Order: Special Victims Unit* plays around the clock.

I'll lie down to read the *Calvin and Hobbes* Margaret loaned me, or the juicy *Gone Girl* knockoff Brooke brought, but I can't focus. For me, Ice-T musing about rape-y murderers (and the murdery ways they raped) is not therapeutic, and it runs—I wish I were kidding—from around 9 a.m. to 10 p.m.

When I'm not gazing covetously at Apartment Man, I'm gazing covetously at the former smoking area, a remnant from some unspecified before-time for this building. Right off the dining room are big windows that look out onto a covered porch, and it looks like paradise. It has a green semitransparent roof, is surrounded by bushes, and is often in shade, which gives it the appearance of being in the rainforest canopy. So, so lush and cool.

There are worn, smooth-looking benches around the perimeter. *The ashtrays are still there.* I have never wanted anything as badly as I want to go out there and smoke 14 cigarettes, but it's locked up now, forever.

"Look," I tell the resident physician, who appears to be 16, "I have never, ever wanted anything like I want to go out there. I've never wanted a man like this."

He has a neutral expression but seems a little curious as to what might be coming next. I continue.

"And, do you smoke? No? Yeah, that's makes sense. Okay, well, all of us who *do* smoke, that tortures us. It's so hard to know that other people had it and we don't. Also, the secure transport guys *told* me I could smoke here, and so far *no one* has let me. And if we can't go out there, they should just paint over the windows so we don't have to stare at what we can't have all day."

He says he's so sorry he can't help me, and I tell him that being that close to something you want with all your heart is worse than never knowing there was a smoker's paradise in the first place.

The food is bad, bad, bad. Everything is the wrong texture, somehow rubbery and runny at the same time. The descriptions make the food sound great, but, like cruise ships, the only thing they can consistently nail is something made far away from here, like English muffins or the orange Yoplaits that are always available to us in a mini-fridge. Eggs are the worst, but nothing is okay. There is a brown sauce, always the same one, appearing in many different dishes.

We are so comically protected from ourselves. We have these soft, stubby little pens (the better to not jab into our or anyone else's veins), and we have to ask a staff member to unlock the bathrooms in our room. The week before I arrived, the health authority decided someone could possibly injure or hang themselves with the bathroom door joint. So now no one gets to pee without staff supervision. This is especially problematic for elderly patients in the middle of the night. It is also a huge burden on the staff, which now have new, time-consuming chores to carry out for each patient. No one likes this.

Several times a day, I must wait quietly and patiently to tell an adult that I have to pee. Along with my hatred of rooms I must be let out of, I now add bathrooms that I must be let into.

No one can charge their phone because we cannot be trusted with anything thin and long; perhaps it would be too tempting to put them around our necks. That last principle limits so much—necklaces, art supplies, the ability to have a fully charged device. I am so, so annoyed by this, even though this rule is designed to thwart the exact behavior that landed me here.

I have no idea what they are plugging our phones into when we hand them over, but something is quite wrong with it. I will surrender my phone, my precious and only source of stimulus, for *hours*, and it comes back with a 34 percent charge. I want to scream and run around and knock things over.

But I don't. I try to be really polite. Here, you bundle all your requests to deliver at once, like you would for a server who has too many tables. You will do this many, many times per day because *every single thing* you want must be granted to you by someone else. I feel like a loon, trying to square the polite thing (not asking someone to address 17 of your needs/wants at once) with the knowledge that I actually don't have any choice in the matter. That's life in the Balkans, baby!

"Hello! So, a couple things. I was hoping I could get a cup of ice and another cup of ice but with coffee poured into it, and also I was wondering if you could charge my phone, please, and I have lost the little pen I had—do you have another one? Can I have some Nicorette? What about a spoon? Oh, also I have to go to the bathroom. Thank you! I'm sorry. Thank you!"

Scattered throughout the ward are many velour posters of quotes misattributed to Albert Einstein, who I am fairly sure said nothing about missing 100 percent of the shots you don't take.

The guy who colored in most of the posters—who looks, more than anyone here, like an upper-middle-class Nike executive—is moving on to a group home after almost a year here (*what, how??*), and this is a nice cause for celebration. I wonder what his life was like before this, and where he is going.

Sam is coming every day, sometimes twice. He is being a saint. He asks me what I would like to eat and then brings it to me; I remember the big luscious shrimp on a salad, briny and cool, with thin slices of crisp, early summer vegetables, and not even a hint of brown sauce. He gets me Bluetooth headphones at Best Buy so I can listen to something besides *SVU*.

But . . . it's not good. He is here, but he is not. He clearly doesn't want to see me; I sense anger that I don't understand roiling inside him. And truth be told, I don't want to see him, either, because he doesn't want to talk to me. He wants, I guess, to sit in silence, and shuts down every conversational balloon I float. If either of us were being even slightly honest with ourselves and each other, we would have been able to see that as toxic as things had been, they had now become unfixably broken by trauma.

I cannot cope with his anger toward me. I wish, so much, that he would just be happy that I'm alive, that he would treat me gently, that he would not silently seethe, and that if he did have to do that, that he would just let me be. He has a right to be angry. But I cannot bear it. I do not understand my own actions, I do not recognize myself or my life and I feel out to sea, the shore receding quickly from view.

But something truly astonishing is happening: the doctors put me back on Wellbutrin, the only antidepressant that has ever truly worked for me, and I am feeling so, so good. Not manic— legitimately content and calm.

In the hospital, rather than taking six weeks to slowly up the dose, they can get you up to speed very quickly while monitoring you for any side effects. By the third or fourth day, I'm cracking jokes with the nurses and my fellow patients, I'm doing little bits of yoga in my room, I'm making a list of things I would like to do this summer just for me, like go on a solo road trip in the Miata. A strange feeling begins welling up within me, and I realize that, under the least likely of circumstances, I am *happy*. This is legitimately the wildest part of the whole experience. For the first time in a year, I feel like being alive.

In retrospect, this isn't actually that crazy: if you go to a hospital and you get very good treatment, you *should* feel a lot better afterward. It's just a pity that I almost had to die for that to happen.

On my last morning in the psych ward, I'm having some *real* challenges adding color to my modular origami sphere. This is the only craft I am able to do. No needles, no thread, and no embroidery floss, of course; no pens that I could dismantle and hurt myself with; and no toxic paints that I could eat or stain a floor with. Yet this is perhaps my most meditative craft. There is no thinking to be done, as each unit is exactly the same. My only job is to make each of the 13 folds as perfectly as I can, and then do it again, 29 times more.

This origami sphere is a replacement for last night's sphere, which was stolen from the nurses' station between 1 and 7 a.m. by Gene. Gene has a lovely, quiet solidity to him; a long braid down his back; and a wolf shirt that feels entirely earned and appropriate.

He's been here for months and months. This is *unfathomable* to me.

Sphere One was discovered in Gene's room around 9:30 a.m., but the occupational therapist made a sad, loving face and said he was *really* treasuring it, that it was prominently displayed in his room among his art and tribal icons. Gene is one of my favorites in the ward, and if it makes *him* happy, *I'm* happy to make another one.

I have asked for and received another eight sheets of computer paper, my morning meds, Nicorette gum, a big cup of that perfect crunchy hospital ice, "iced coffee" that is one part hospital coffee to four parts aforementioned ice now melted, supervised use of the bathroom, and a spork for breakfast.

One by one, I fold and tear each piece of paper into a square and then tear that square into four smaller squares until I have 32, which I stack to my left. With each square, I fold two corners to the center, each new edge to the center again. I square off the ends into a little burrito, fold each tip northwest into a point, and then accordion-fold the entire enterprise. I carefully tuck pointed ends into tight pockets, gathering the soft peaks together until the last piece is in.

I learned to make this sphere in eighth grade at a "Super Saturday," which was something my school district put on for out-of-place children like myself in lieu of actual gifted and talented programming. Super Saturdays, which happened at the other middle school in town, consisted of weirdo community members teaching their weirdo skills to weirdo youths, and I *loved* it. A typical Super Saturday might include a make-your-own-shadow-puppet workshop; Learn the Science of Wind!; an advanced math or physics class for the truly brilliant and tortured; and, on one especially super Super Saturday, modular origami, in which you fold many of the same unit and then fashion them together into an elaborate whole.

And here I am, more than 20 years later, still making these things, which are technically known as stellated icosahedrons (a.k.a. pointy origami spheres). They live on. Not just in my brain, either, but in the homes of many people I currently or formerly loved.

Now, I'm making it for the nurses who have been so kind, who have cracked jokes with me, and who have given me a couple extra vaporwave insulated cups to enjoy at home.

I'm making it for Gene, who has been here for months already and will probably be here for months to come.

I'm making it for myself, to stay busy. To stay engaged. To stay alive.

Sonobe Module Stellated Icosahedron
(a.k.a. Origami Spheres)

The stellated icosahedron is my hat trick of crafting, insofar as it's neat, it takes a while but not *too* long, the recipient has almost certainly never seen anything like it, and it's very light and compact. I have made it for friends and boyfriends and girlfriends and therapists and coworkers and mentors. It says, "Here. I sat down and hunched over and put my face eight inches above the table for, like, two hours straight. I made this because I love you, and I'm hoping this strange thing proves it."

Materials:

- Origami paper (You'll want 3 pieces for a tiny double-pyramid thing, 6 for a cube, 12 for a small ball, or 30 for the one mentioned here.)

Instructions:

1. Go to YouTube, search for "Sonobe module tutorial," and watch a video.

2. After you've watched it and mastered the module itself (which is very simple, as far as origami goes), watch a few more videos on how to connect the units together.

3. I'm sorry. I really, really tried to write this all out in a way that

makes sense, but I promise that trying to follow written direc-
tions on this will only bring you grief. Just like I learned this
from watching someone, you're going to have to as well.

When I'm done, I hold, as always, a pointy little ball, light but
surprisingly intact. You can gently toss it in the air and catch it or
spin it lightly on a table. Normally, these go on a shelf or side table
or in a cubicle hutch, and I'll see them from time to time and feel
happy that I know this person, that they are in my life, that they
like this dumb dorky thing I made.

I do not want to see this one ever again.

I mean, I definitely won't literally see it again (that thing
probably had a half-life of about eight hours), but I don't think
I'll figuratively see it again, either, because I'm getting discharged
today.

My suicide attempt was, as a doctor in the psychiatric hospital
told my mother, a hideous fluke.

"I don't believe she's a suicidal person," the psychiatrist said.
"I'm honestly not that worried about her going forward. It was just
this perfect storm."

I'm not sure I believe him—and my mom definitely has some
doubts—but I'm ready to get some agency back and leave this
place behind. I'm supposed to be discharged at 11:15 this morning. Now, it is 9:43, and time is moving so, so slowly. Now it's
10:12. Now 10:24. 10:30. 10:47. 10:53. 11. I am vibrating.

I give my Bluetooth headphones to my roommate, and she
seems genuinely touched. We each wish each other luck, and hug.

Now, I'm getting a big clear bag with all the things I wasn't allowed to have with me—phone chargers and pens and jewelry and a comb with a pointy end—and now I am being walked through big locking doors into the lobby where I first checked in. That was four days ago but feels like four months.

Sam is here waiting for me, and I am over the moon. I am seeing in 10,000 new colors, hearing in four dimensions—the world has never, ever looked so beautiful to me. As we swing onto 99E, I can see Portland spread out ahead of me—bridges and buildings and on-ramps and off-ramps and everywhere people just doin' their thing! It's like *The Busy World of Richard Scarry*, and I am moved almost to tears. I am so in love with all of it that I do not notice that beside me, Sam is silent with rage.

CHAPTER 9

Well . . . ish

In Which I Gain a Lot of Sanity
and Lose a Lot of Mobility

IT'S ALWAYS SHOCKING WHEN MEDICAL INTERVENTION works precisely as it's supposed to and all a sudden you are well . . . ish.

I was gleeful with freedom. I cleaned Sam's entire house because guess who now was allowed to use a broom *and* a dustpan?! Guess who could open (most) doors if she wanted and could leave a room when *she* felt like leaving?!? These incredible privileges plus the medication left me extremely hyped on life. When Eleanor saw me, she yelped with joy and almost vibrated apart, and I felt the exact same way.

I hadn't realized how very dark and small my world had become. I'd dropped each joy, one by one, not noticing they were gone or really remembering I'd had them at all. I stopped listening to music, stopped dancing, stopped going on country drives. I stopped enjoying food, found no pleasure in good company, but instead a temporary lessening of misery, which made me a superfun presence. Depression is so talented at turning you from a foodie into someone who wishes they could just eat a compressed nutrition bar every day, except about *everything*.

I started to do and fall in love with all my favorite activities again, with gusto. I remembered what it was to put a new song I loved on repeat, to make little involuntary happy noises when biting into a soft ball of burrata, to push the Miata to 6,000 rpms, to rewrite Carly Rae Jepsen lyrics to be about my dog, to put on heels and a slip to mop while "Dangerous Woman" plays out of the speakers at full volume.

I made myself a whiteboard with a grid titled, "But what have you done LATELY?" Each day, I could check off small, achievable things I knew were good for me—texting a friend I'd lost contact with, spending 15 minutes organizing, or doing a little bit of yoga.

Emily and Carrie were still gone. I didn't hear from them, and I haven't ever since. But I did, slowly, tell some other close girlfriends what had happened and where I'd been. I made efforts to get dates on the calendar, just to see each other and talk. I called my mom almost every day. I did seem to set Sam off more than usual, which I didn't understand. Wasn't he happy I was okay?

I know this sounds a little pat. It's not like I left the hospital okay, at all, and also there was the not-small matter of my life being in complete shambles.

But the medication worked miraculously well for me, and it felt like breaking through to the surface. Unlike the medication that sent me into a mania, this one instead gave me a sense that although I had a long, long road ahead of me, I also had the inner strength to face it. Rather than an overwhelming urge to run from life, I began to see the many tiny beautiful things that comprise it.

I had feelings again! Not only feelings, but *joy*! I felt that I could make my mental health a priority in my life, that I knew how to find help, that I now knew how to keep myself safe. I was able to see, for the first time in years, beyond my pain and out into the world.

I truly do think, now, that depression is like diabetes. Many lifestyle changes can help, but for me, the right medication has to be in place. Otherwise, I'm just not well enough to enact those lifestyle changes.

Originally, the hospital discharged me with a therapist's appointment scheduled two and a half weeks later, to the extreme dismay of my mother and Sam.

This also made the therapist—whom I will call Billy, as he has an Eichneresque energy—*very, very angry*. Honestly, he said, he had always *respected* and *trusted* Unity . . . until now! Now, he said, they were *dumping* me alone in the world! This was *irresponsible*, and a *dereliction of duty*, and he had called *just* to tell them that. I felt a little bad for causing this rift, but I already loved him so much.

He does say that he can't give me the care I need right now: I'd gone from the highest level of care (inpatient and protected full-time) to the lowest one (seeing a therapist), and there was no point in trying to unpack any trauma until I was fully stabilized. So we spent the appointment calling around to find a psychiatrist who had a place for me and would accept my insurance. Once I was under a medical doctor's care and my brain was well and truly stabilized, then and only then would Billy let me come back to him.

I did, and he did, and today I see Billy regularly for ongoing mental health care, and I love him. He doesn't scream *"No!"* when I say something we both know is bullshit, but he will say, *"Stop.*

Stop. I do not believe that *even one bit*, and we *both* know *you don't either."* He possesses the very best therapist quality: he's way, way too smart for me to snow and makes this apparent at every turn. He bosses me around a little bit but in good ways. Also, we often talk about *Vanderpump Rules* because, as he notes, anything can be therapeutic.

But it would be quite a while until he felt that therapy was an appropriate level of care for me. For now, it was an intensive out-patient program next to a dead mall where I once attended a Girl Scout lock-in.

Three days a week, for three hours a day, I go to a hospital's Behavioral Wellness Center to sit in a room with maybe 12 people—oriented and not—and talk about how, if you feel a panic attack coming on, you can look around the room and begin count-ing colors. I see one, two, three, four . . . etc., blues and how many oranges?

In my mind, I was acing this bad boy, just like I'd crushed it in the psychiatric hospital. I had my hand up so many times with insights!

One day, we were talking about how to make our houses safe for ourselves—and I stuck my hand up.

"What about a big box of the people who love you? Like pic-tures and letters and such, and if you were feeling very bad you could go look at that and call one of those people?"

"I love it!" the therapist said. (Not my Billy, but rather my as-signed counselor for the program.) He asked if I worked in "the industry," and once again I got to smugly reply that *no,* I'm actually an *author,* but I've done *a lot of work in the space,* and then he ex-claimed a little bit about how cool it is I'm a writer and I got to flirt with him in the lowest-stakes way one must flirt with a therapist.

My psychiatrist there was a compact and stunningly beautiful man whose suits left me flummoxed. They were that good. He'd arrive in a bottle-blue number with a perfect peach pocket square and cognac-colored shoes that looked like they cost more than my mortgage because they did. I googled, "Can patients date their doctors?" but tragically, the psychiatrist-patient is the one type of doctor-patient relationship that is strictly verboten even *after* the professional relationship has terminated. Boo!*

He talked to me for an hour and a half the first time we met, which is certainly the longest I've ever talked to a doctor about anything. He asked me about my past; about how I worked; about how the mania had felt; about what my experiences of happiness, ennui, and sadness are like. He asked me about my family, my relationships, the nature of the ones I'd lost, the nature of the ones who remained.

He told me that one of the most difficult clinical distinctions to make is between women who have ADHD and depression versus women who have ADHD and bipolar II disorder. The hyperfocus and intensity of ADHD looks a lot like the hypomania of bipolar (which is much milder than what we often think of as mania). In fact, he said, many if not most of the creatives he works with who have had success in their careers and assume they have depression are, in fact, bipolar. He couldn't say for sure in my case—there's no blood test—but the only way to tell would be if I had another manic episode in my life.

I've gotten a diagnosis or two in my day, starting with ADHD when I was very young, depression in my teens, and generalized

---

*Look, I know this makes it seem like I was horned up for my behavioral health team, and *maybe I was!* It was a weird summer.

anxiety disorder in my early 20s. There are also some that I never officially got but probably qualified for during years of disordered eating.

But none hit me like this. For whatever reason, I was fine with ADHD/depressed/anxious/sometimes being very, very bad at food. But *this*? This was a bridge too far! This was *Girl, Interrupted* territory. I'd finally felt comfortable talking about depression and anxiety, but this made me feel so shameful, so unfixably broken.

If you're thinking that this is a stunningly hypocritical thing for someone who is comfortable with her and others' mental health struggles, and also absurd coming from someone who had to be hospitalized while in a mania, well: yes.

But like so many people, I had a wildly incorrect view of what bipolar depression looked like compared with unipolar depression. People often think of bipolar I disorder, which tends to have much more pronounced manias. Bipolar II's highs are hypomania, not full-blown mania, and can just look like someone feeling happy and productive. Many times, people with bipolar II don't get diagnosed because their highs may never have caused problems or even been noticed.

Plus, those highs are rare. My doctor told me that 39 out of 40 times, when a female with bipolar II is emotionally dysregulated, she's in depression, not hypomania.

There was another difficult possibility in here for me: looking back on my life, there have been times of enormous creativity and productivity. I usually find myself snapping into this mode when a deadline nears, and endless words pour forth from me. During these times, I feel funnier than usual, more alive, and in some cases almost magical. I achieve enormous things that I didn't believe I could, and this gives me a confidence, even when I am completely in darkness. Is this part of me, which I treasure so much, just a manifestation of mental illness?

To date, I haven't had another hypomania. For a while, I took mood stabilizers, but I went off them with my doctor's blessing and have felt no different. Maybe I have a tendency toward bipolar II, or maybe I have depression and ADHD, which, again, can cause a lot of what I described earlier. But in the end, it doesn't matter. As my psychiatrist put it, the diagnosis itself isn't the important part. The important part is finding the care and treatment that lets me live a happy, healthy life, and I'm so insanely grateful that I have.

The intensive outpatient work took up three days a week, but I was ready for more and began looking for a part-time job. Not a work-from-home, by-myself job: one with a workplace that I had to get dressed for, and people who I would work with and be accountable to.

I was probably too feral for full-time work at that point, but nor did I trust myself to get back to writing—I was still too fragile to make meaningful career moves and/or put down anything permanently, which is sort of the whole thing with writing.

By weird chance, Kate Spade hung herself around the time I was released from the hospital, with Anthony Bourdain doing the same a few days later. I was *sure* that this was a sign I should write all about this—even though I had not been out of the hospital for a full week at this point. I called one of my best friends, who is an editor, to pitch this and, thank *God*, she very gently suggested that it sounded like I needed to process a bit more first.

But I needed to do something. I wanted to get out of the house, work with other people, and hopefully move around a lot. I wanted something that would allow me to engage and learn new things. I wanted a reason to get off the couch.

I set my sights on two jobs. I wanted very much to work in the paint or lighting department of the North Salem Home Depot, one of my very favorite places. Oh, how I love that Home Depot! Each department has an old-timer named Bob or Barb who is gonna tell you exactly what you're gonna need to do; positive gay teenagers make up at least 25 percent of the staff; and everyone's always hanging out on those orange half-ladders together, having the best time. Also, just imagine how much I would've learned about home maintenance!*

The other option was pouring wine at a winery, which is a not-uncommon job here in the mid-Willamette Valley (or, more precisely, the Eola-Amity Hills American Viticulture Area). I love wine and know a bit about it; I love, love, love working in the service industry; and blathering on while strangers politely listen is one of my truest joys.

Home Depot wanted me to begin work at 5 a.m., so that was out. But the first winery I stopped at, the marketing manager remembered me from my newspaper days. We chatted for a bit, and I left with instructions to return the following Saturday.

The winery was small and exquisitely beautiful. There was a little tasting room, but the main action was outside, where Adirondack chairs and shaded tables were scattered in a beautiful white poplar grove. People played lawn games, kids ran around, and I learned and then explained all sorts of things: biodynamicism and barrels and soil and terroir and malolactic fermentation.

I truly feel like I've turned a corner and am going to be okay.**

---

* The ultimate craft?

** Lol.

✂

I should have moved it. But that's not how life works, is it? I walked past that round peg on the ground two or three times, and thought, *That's not where that goes. Put it in its little crate with the rest of the game*, and then I'd realize this table needed wiping, or that person had yet to try the 2014 Reserve Pinot.

I had, in fact, just poured that very pinot to an interesting couple I wanted to be friends with. I had *so* much to say about its complicated, dark, spicy nature that I was *still* looking at and talking to them as I walked away.

"So actually, right at the end you get a little bit of tobacco smokiness, but—"

I stepped on the peg, rolled my ankle all the way under my foot, and was down on the ground, unable to finish my thought.

I was trying so, so hard not to make any noise and pretend that this was a just-for-fun, casual fall and I actually *wanted* to be right here in the dirt, holding onto my ankle for no reason.

The illusion was undermined by the fact that I could not get up and was silently crying. The sweet couple were stricken, and he—a former EMT—rushed over to try to assess the situation. I could not bear any weight, but I was positive it was just a bad sprain. I asked them what they'd thought of the 2014, and they looked at me with naked pity.

"It was . . . good," he said, looking confused about the entire pretext of this conversation. "Yeah. So, should we . . . Do you want to go to the hospital?"

My boss brought me a big glass of wine, which I gulped down because I was now clearly off the clock. I texted Sam, and he texted something brief and curt back. I did not know that, along with my fibula, the fall had permanently shattered the relationship for reasons that I would only understand months later.

Ever the resistant patient, I kept trying to get up and "walk it off." When Sam arrived, I insisted we go to urgent care instead of the hospital because I could not admit to myself that something was—again and per fucking usual—very wrong with my body.

Sam took me to the hospital, driving silently, not responding to my attempts at conversation. *Why is he so mad at me? Does he think I fell and hurt my ankle at him?* I try to cheerfully engage, but it goes nowhere.

I was getting out of the car and into a wheelchair when a giant truck with ATVs in the back screeched to a halt behind us. A giant man popped out, sprinted around to the passenger side, and opened the back cab door. An even larger man was inside, screaming. Just screaming. So loud. Screaming, screaming, screaming—pausing for breath—screaming some more.

You would not believe how uncomfortable it is to listen to a large, grown man hollering in pain at full volume. It is blood-curdling.

"AHHHHHHHHHHHHH! JESUS CHRIST!! AHH-HHHHHHHHHHHHH! AHHHHHHHHHHHHHHHH-HHHHHH! AAAAH! AAAH! AAAAH! FUCK!!!!!!! AHHHHHHHHHHHHH!"

Sam and I stopped and gawked. Someone hustled out with a stretcher, and several staff members gingerly transferred and then strapped the man to it, as he continued to make chilling, affecting noises that set off a mammalian panic.

Sam went to park, and I wheeled myself inside. The gal at the front desk was sweet, saying ruefully that they were having a super-slow day and would see me soon but obviously needed to deal with *that*—she nodded in the direction the man had disappeared—first.

Of course. No problem, I get it. I wheeled myself into the lobby and waited patiently.

Someone (the wife? girlfriend?) of Yelling Man was standing nearby sobbing.

"Hey, I'm so sorry," I said. "Honestly, it's a *really good* sign that he's yelling like that because if he wasn't, it would be a super-bad sign."

She looked at me and nodded, sniffling. Sam joined me in the lobby but would not make eye contact; when they called my name, he didn't come back to the room with me, even though I asked him to.

An hour or two later, I was leaving with my ankle in a splint and instructions to visit an orthopedic surgeon ASAP because—

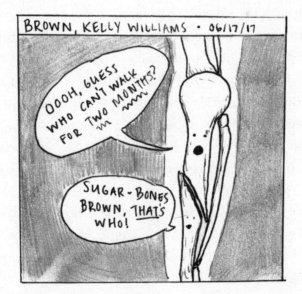

and I'm sure you didn't see this coming—I have a spiral fracture of my fibula. From walking. Walking across a goddamn lawn.

I giggle a haunted laugh when they tell me this.

Of course! Of *course* it is broken. Of *course* it happened on day five of the job I'd gotten to free myself from Depression Couch. *Of fucking course.* I want to push something over, something that will make a huge clatter. I want to scream and scream like Yelling Man did.

And then, because I am afraid of my own anger, unwilling or unable to just feel shitty about things, I told myself that it was *fine*, although even as I thought it, I knew it wouldn't be. Lying to yourself can be a great momentary coping mechanism; a lie you tell yourself sincerely can be the only thing that lets you approach hope.

I could not bear, in that moment, to admit to myself what was happening because I knew exactly how bad it would be, although I wondered how this would compare to the familiar ol' broken arm. On the downside, it seemed like not walking would be tough; on the upside, I could still masturbate.

Then, a small miracle. Somewhere within me a little voice peeped up. Unlike the self-pity and self-deception that were swirling, it said the thing I most needed to hear: *You can handle this. You will be okay. It will suck, terribly, but you will move past it, and it will just be another funny-horrible detail of this time in your life. This is not like it was before. Now, you can handle it because your brain is okay. After what you have been through, nothing is ever going to be that hard again.**

And, I tell myself, at least I'm not that fuckin' ATV dude. That sounded god-awful. Wonder what happened to that guy?

---

* As of August 2020, this remains true.

"Hey," I said, twisting in my seat to face the nurse who was wheeling me out. "I know you're not, like, supposed to tell me this, but—is that guy gonna be okay?"

The faintest shadow of a smirk passed over his face.

"Yeah. He's gonna be fine."

"But . . . he is injured, right?"

"No, yeah, he's injured. But he's going to be fine."

This, obviously, was a relief. Then, a subversive thought: "But is he hurt *worse* than me?"

"Nope. About the same. In fact, exactly the same."

I am agog. The *audacity* of some men! Men who think so much of themselves that they can just scream and scream, ruining everyone's afternoon! Who, when they are in pain, do not care that the sounds of their voice is making strangers want to cry! Who take themselves so seriously that they get strapped down to a stretcher and run into the ER for a *broken ankle*. *I* broke *my* ankle first! Why did he get to go ahead of me? Why did *I* comfort *his* girlfriend when he was taking *my* turn in the X-ray?

It never occurred to me that maybe the question I should ask wasn't "Why is he being so loud?" but rather "Why am I being so quiet?"

✂

Speaking of quiet, Sam continues to be livid, and I continue to not have a fucking clue what in God's name is wrong with him, a sentiment I express fully.

By the time we get to my house, we have already had a screaming fight—about what, I cannot begin to remember—and rather than letting him help me, I pull myself across the backyard like poor Christina from that Andrew Wyeth painting; the level of pathos is stratospheric. *"Fuck you, I'll crawl on the lawn rather than hold onto someone who yells at his girlfriend for breaking her ankle. Why are you yelling at me? Please be nice! I NEED YOU TO BE NICE! My fucking ankle is broken, can you PLEASE just be NICE?"*

When I finally get inside, I am pulling myself to the bathroom across the hardwood floor, and it is *fucking filthy*. This is its near-constant state, with giant Eleanor-fur tumbleweeds blowing everywhere.

Let me tell you something about the floor in my house, the air, the furniture, the nooks, everything I own, and the very atoms around me: it's all Eleanor fur. Upstairs, downstairs, in the basement, in the yard, at my desk in the office, in an Irish hotel room: Eleanor fur.

It's an incredible substance. The hairs are bright white and eight inches long but look like they've all been crimped. They are always, somehow, in my mouth or eyes, hampering my contacts or under my tongue.

She probably creates a fully stuffed gallon Ziploc bag's worth per month. It roams around my house in potato-sized tumbleweeds. It can never be truly contained, only contended with.

I have accepted this fur as inextricable from the being of Eleanor, so theoretically, it's a divine substance because my dog is a perfect angel who can do no wrong. I know that there will be years when I'd give anything—*anything*—to have her fur woven sturdily through every item of clothing I own and also somehow in the barbecue chicken my neighbor is serving me. But also, sometimes, it makes me feel like a filthy human who, no matter what, cannot get things clean.

The floor is covered with her hair, now collecting on my splint, so I start crying at my past self's failure to deal with it and then ask Sam if he will please sweep the floor.

Let me tell you this: Sam is what has been standing between my house and chaos, consistently, for *months*. Sam swept my house constantly, and is a man uniquely dedicated to floor cleanliness. But today, he is done with that just like he is done with me.

"I don't *want* to sweep the fucking floor."

"Well, *I sure as fuck can't sweep it!*" I wail at him, dissolving into fresh hysterics, doing a gasping-sobbing thing. "PLEASE—SWEEP—THE—FLOOR!"

He glares at me, storms into the kitchen, grabs the broom, and starts sweeping the floor in showy rage. It actually would've been really funny if it were an *SNL* sketch and not, y'know, what I months later would recognize as the end of my relationship.

This is not the most flattering portrayal of Sam, and it was certainly not his finest afternoon. But what I didn't understand—and wouldn't for a long time after—was that he just had nothing left.

"Everything, for months, had been *all about helping you*, constantly," he told me later. "You *in* the hospital, you *out* of the hospital, you when you got your *purse* stolen, you when Carrie and Emily weren't around, you and your dad, you, you, *you*, and now it was you assuming that, once *again*, I would drop every single thing in my life and rearrange it to wait on you hand and foot. And I just couldn't. *I wasn't okay*, and there was no one to help me, ever."

He had indeed supported me, in ways successful and not, through so much. I took it for granted, as though I were owed it. We were two very flawed people who were trying our best to help each other but also failing miserably.

All I could think about was how, before all this, he'd told me I was the best thing that had ever happened to him, that he was terrified of losing me, that he wanted to be better, and could I please be patient with him? And I had been a good girlfriend, I really had. I could not square in my mind that he both loved me deeply and that he couldn't look at me. I was so full of my own grasping need that I couldn't address or maybe even see his, and vice versa.

><

A week and a half later, I am in significantly less pain. I've gotten myself a knee scooter, a backpack, and an office chair—the Holy Trinity of the broken-ankled—and I'm slowly figuring out the contours of this exhausting new life. I am optimistic that I will be walking within a week or so.

This delusion is shattered by my first visit to the orthopedic surgeon.

"Well, we're *definitely* looking at surgery!" he says cheerfully as he enters the room. What? *What?* What? Like, with screws and a plate? That's for people who shatter their ankles in a car accident! I tripped on a lawn game! I rolled my ankle. *It should be sprained.*

I share this reasoning with him, but it does not change his mind about whether or not I need surgery.

"What if I refuse to get it?" I say, demonstrating the same helpful, cooperative energy I've brought to every medical professional who has tried to take care of me these past two years.

He looks faintly amused.

"Okay, so!" he says, and beckons me over to look at an X-ray. "You see these three little bones, and how they meet right there? Well if this one," he points to a tiny knob, "heals more than five millimeters out of place, you lose about half of the structural stability of your ankle."

"Which would mean . . . ?"

"Which would mean you'll just keep rolling and dislocating and breaking your ankle again and again," he says, and leans back and puts his hands behind his head, as though this settles the matter. Which it sort of does.

The surgery really is miraculous—if this had happened any time except in the past 80 years, I'd just have a sad, Tiny Tim foot for the rest of my life, flopping around and breaking again and again until I mercifully died of an unrelated UTI. Instead, I now have a plate and seven screws that are relatively parallel, and I get to ask people if they want to touch the plate and feel the screws—a *really* polarizing question. People can really surprise you with their answers! *And, someday, I will get to walk.*

But that day, I did not have the emotional capacity for these compassionate, grateful thoughts. Instead, I was just full of impotent rage—at what? At a lawn. At myself and my brain and my body. At Carrie. At Sam. At Trump, always looming in the background like a malevolent Macy's Thanksgiving Day Parade balloon. At my surgeon. At my mother. At my dog and her fur. At my dad and his cancer. At my inability to do even a single thing for myself, while every other person in the world still gets to get up and walk around on their two fucking feet.

But most of all, I'm still so angry at God. Not even angry, really, just so, so hurt and bewildered. I feel like God kicked me in the teeth. God saw me happy and decided I still didn't deserve it, even after everything. *I had gotten this job specifically to get out of my house that was trapping me—and now I can't leave it for two months.* On my fifth fucking shift. For more than a year, a psychological barrier made it nearly impossible for me to leave my house. Just as I'd finally slipped free and remembered how beautiful it can be out there, I am trapped again, but this time physically.

So You Can't Walk!

Once upon a time, you were able to just, say, decide you want some grapes and execute quickly on that plan. No more! Now, it is up to you to relearn pretty much every way you move through the world. Here are my very best tips:

- Get a knee scooter ASAP, and make sure it has a basket. Crutches are impossible and awful, although they're slightly better if you order pads for them online.

- Get a backpack because this is literally the only way you can move something from place to place. Keep your backpack organized, too. I made sure to always have my phone, keys, wallet, medical paperwork, phone chargers, and a power bank in mine.

- For the kitchen, you're going to want an office chair on wheels that can be adjusted upward or downward. You can sit on it and scoot around to the fridge or the sink, which makes meal prep a million times easier.

- If you've been told to elevate, get a purpose-made elevation pillow online. They're far sturdier than trying to stack a bunch of pillows, and you can actually sleep with your leg up on them. If you are told to elevate, *elevate every single second you are not moving* because it makes a huge difference.

- Remember that you really only have the energy to do about one thing per day. Going *anywhere*, even just popping in to a convenience store, is a Thing. You will then need to go home and rest for several hours, so save yourself the frustration of scheduling and then canceling things.

- Any change in elevation (even just a few inches) is truly, truly difficult. Get used to scooting up and down stairs on your butt. Thank every single being in the universe for the ADA, because low-grade ramps are now your liberation.

I'd set aside big chunks of my summer to take care of my dad as he went through radiation and chemo, plus used a feeding tube. Caretaking is grueling work, but I was grateful that I *could* do it, and that perhaps I'd be able to give back to one of my parents even a fraction of the care and love he gave me through my life.

Now, of course, that is right out and I am in the market for a caretaker myself. My mother steps up because Sam needed space—he is texting me sometimes but not nearly as often as I'm texting him, and soon he goes to visit his family across the country. Mom moves me into her home for the first few days after the surgery, when I can't move at all. Luckily, she's a teacher and is on summer break and I post up on the couch, asking her for every single thing I need. Once again, I bundle my requests: "Could you please bring the extension cord over here so I can plug in my phone, and also the phone charger, and also can I have some water, and if you are in the fridge anyway, a snack? Wait, here's some garbage, can you throw these balled-up Kleenexes away? Thank you! I'm sorry! Thank you!"

This is the second time in as many months that I cannot get

myself a glass of water. All I want is to be able to take care of myself, which is *exactly* what I was finally doing. I'd felt such insane freedom when I left the hospital, and yet here I am again, unable to walk through doors.

My mom and I remind each other about once an hour what great sports we're being. And we really are! My mother is the best one in the world, but she is not one of those moms who is so obsessed with her children that any time is precious, and even if she was, this time sucks. By now, she's spent nearly every day of her summer vacation tending to her fragile, abject child. Meanwhile, I am so, so tired of being a fragile, abject child.

I love my mother so deeply. We each have our quirks, but our relationship is uncomplicated. We call each other for advice, we talk on the phone about nothing for hours, she makes me laugh until I pee and vice versa—she is a uniquely satisfying and wonderful mother.

That summer, her love is perhaps the main thing (besides medication) that keeps me afloat and makes me feel like I can do it. She is conspicuously *not* sorry for me, which I truly appreciate. When I start to complain (as I often do), she points out that I am going to be able to walk again, and a lot of people don't. If I say I'm not sure I'll ever write or date again, she tells me that's ridiculous, and this helps me realize how temporary my state is. Most of all, in a time when I question whether I am worthy of love and care, she again and again tells me with her actions that I am.

So of course I am terrified of losing her. And that terror morphs into some particularly morbid crafting.

✂

Comics to Confront Your Mother's Mortality

I'll tell you something: I do not care one bit for skeletons, generally speaking. Here's a noninclusive list of complaints:

- There's this weird rigid structure inside all of us at all times, almost as hard as stone, covered with bloody musculature *and* consciousness. If you mention this as small talk, you're going to upset everyone.

- Why must there be so *many* bones? Of varying sizes and shapes? There are literally hundreds! Some of them look like a five-year-old's drawing of a bone, some of them look like little tiny pebbles, and some of them cover your brain but can also be made into a goblet. The entire affair is disorganized.

- It's weird that they're both load-bearing *and* making blood. This feels like mission creep.

My skeleton is technically doing things for me all the time, but I only actively interface with it when something has gone wrong. The only time I really discuss my—or anyone else's—skeleton is when an attractive orthopedic surgeon with a thick neck is frowning at pictures of mine and laying out a very long timeline.

Besides my dog,* the most troubling mortality in my life belongs to my mother. Doing a comic of her just sort of living her life,

---

* Who is going to live forever. No follow-up questions at this time, thank you.

THE GOOD
HYDRANGEA

THE BAD
HYDRANGEA

but as a skeleton, felt like a good way to explore these feelings while also implying that my mother will still be fretting about Christmas decorations from beyond the grave.

This acknowledges that she's someday going to die and then makes that inevitability familiar. It says to Death, "Whatever, you're real, and I am powerless in your face. Fine. I'm going to doodle my mother existing and enduring as herself beyond you because she will."

This is perhaps my central coping mechanism. Whatever it is, I'm going to laugh at it and take away its power (or at least feel like I have). I am going to take the worst thing and make it into something I can love, or at least survive with.

Anyway, I highly recommend making gentle humor comics about something you find terrifying. Here are a few ideas to get you started:

- An enormous spider lives in your house, because it is your older sister. It has some good advice for you but also stays in a relationship that's not abusive, per se, but certainly is way beyond its expiration date and toxic for all involved.

- The devil has a part-time job at your coffee shop of choice. He seems to be doing his best, having recently graduated from Michigan. He's actually the first college grad in his family! He's dedicated to spreading evil across the earth to bring about the downfall of humanity but also is pretty excited for the opportunity to work in his field, which is PR.

- You are a ghost but still attending parties your friends throw.

- The world has ended and cannibalism runs rampant, but your dad has all the same concerns about how often you're changing your oil.

Materials:

- Paper (I often use black paper for Skelemom—I do it in white ink—but you can use a sketchbook or even printer paper. Who cares? This is for you!)
- A hard pencil for sketching
- A good eraser (Again, and as always, I recommend STAEDTLER Mars.)

- Pens (As noted earlier, I use a white uni-ball, but Micron pens are great for inking, as are brush pens.)
- A straightedge of some sort

Tips:

- Make your dialogue as close as possible to a quote you have heard in person. Usually, Skelemom comics are almost verbatim something my mother has said, or at least *would* say. The familiarity is what makes it funny.

- Decide on your format. One panel? Four? I like to make each one a single illustrated moment, so there's usually not a lot of back-and-forth.

- I do Skelemom in white ink on black paper, but regardless, you'll want to get everything done in pencil first. Sketch very lightly, and erase any mistakes with a soft eraser (*not* the one on the end of the pencil; this only leads to heartbreak). I highly recommend STAEDTLER Mars, which is white with a blue sleeve and available in every art and office supply store.

- Draw and erase liberally, keeping in mind that you can just leave old pencil marks for now if they're not getting in the way.

- I like to put the dialogue down on the page first, because my comics tend to be wordy.

- If the dialogue is really long, I'll practice writing it out on a separate sheet, seeing how many words fit per line and keeping in mind that there are natural breaks between phrases. A simple example:

→ *Good* vs **BAD** DIALOGUE SPACING:

SO THEN I SAID, "WAIT. WHAT IF THIS IS JUST A SIMULATION?

NO.

SO THEN I SAID, "HEY: ARE WE SURE THAT ZEBRAS EXIST?"

Yes!

- Write everything out *and then* draw the bubble around it, rather than the other way around.

- When you write dialogue, write in all caps. It's more legible.

- You'll want a variety of thicknesses of pens to do your outlining. If you're just getting started, I'd have one felt-tip (Paper Mate Flair is great for this), one .7mm, and one .3mm pen for fine detail work (uni-ball Signo is a great and widely available choice; I use this in opaque white on black paper for Skelemom and regular inks for white paper).

- As you trace over your pencil, go slowly. If you have straight lines, use a straightedge (or at least pull toward yourself on the stroke, which I find makes for a straighter line than going away). If you're making a curve or arc, think about leaving the bottom part of your hand down (rest it on a little piece of paper so you don't smudge your comic), keeping your wrist still, and moving your hand in an arc.

- When you're done tracing, erase all the pencil marks. Go over the entire page, thoroughly, because you don't realize how many little pencil marks are still around until they aren't there.

• It doesn't matter if, like Skelemom, only six of your Instagram friends get this at all. It's not for them. This is for you.

✄

Back at my mother's house, I'm figuring out ways to cope. When I want to smoke a cigarette, I scoot my scooter over to the back door and then gently lower myself to sit on the floor. I open the screen door and swing my casted leg through it and then scooch my butt over the threshold until I'm outside on the concrete steps. I can't go too far, though, and if anyone else tries to open the screen door because they don't see me there, I get hit right in the tush.

But despite all of this, I know, deep in my heart, that I'm going to be okay, and this radical thought gets me (slowly) out of bed in the morning. The medication truly has been life-changing, and I find myself optimistic, even. For the first time in who knows how long, I know I have the capacity to weather this. The waters are still so rough, but at least I've managed to climb onto a boat.

People sometimes say they worry medication will make them less of themselves. Of course, I can only speak to my own experience, but to me, it makes me *more* of myself. I feel happy when good things happen and sad when bad things happen.

I am, that summer, terribly sad that I can't walk, that I can't help my father, that I can't do the job I'd been so enjoying, that I hurt Sam so terribly yet cling to him in fear. But I am also able to be happy, to enjoy a meal my mom cooked, to feel so grateful when friends would come visit me and chat for hours.

You should've seen me when I realized I could get upstairs to my bedroom. I'd leave the scooter at the landing and scuttle up the stairs and around the room on my hands and one leg, dragging my casted leg behind me like a deranged Spider-Man. I felt so powerful, so resilient, and so proud of myself.

On the night of my birthday, I stop in 7-Eleven, and a "LINDA" personalized keychain catches my eye. I have earned it.

I celebrate each little success like it's my PhD. When I am allowed to put my cast down and put weight on both feet, you should've *seen* the standing I did! Shifting my weight back and forth between them, like it isn't even a thing, sometimes for up to 10 minutes!

My first out-of-the-house event is to meet some friends for karaoke. I drive downtown, park, carefully swing my scooter out of the car, and almost vibrate my teeth out as I roll my scooter across the bumpy pavement. When I get inside, I set it next to the wall with a note:

"Hello! Please do not steal or move this scooter, as it is really important to me. That said, it's very fun and you're welcome to try it out! Just let the redhead with a ponytail in the floral blue dress know and return it here."

Three people buy me drinks in exchange for scooter time, which is a win if I've ever seen one.

✄

But . . . there is the not-small matter of Sam. From July through October, we have the most protracted, gutting breakup imaginable.

Normally, when I'm done, I'm *done*; if they dump me, my pride doesn't allow for any further contact. But not this time. We *reallllllly* stretch it out. It confuses me because I can tell he still loves me but finds it actively painful to be around me.

When he can stand to be around me, he is so loving. He makes me the most tender nest on his comfy patio couch. He's thought of everything. There is a dog-proof box of snacks and a little tiny cooler full of Diet Coke. There is a little-bitty garbage can and a box to put recycling in. This is *so key* because you cannot possibly understand how many bits of garbage you create until you can't throw them away.

There is an ashtray and a lighter (again, the couch was outside) and a power strip that he plugs my phone and laptop into. There is a Bluetooth speaker and blankets of varying weights. He carefully tucks giant fuzzy socks over my toes where they poke out of the cast because he knows they are always cold.

I know I've fucked him up, but I don't understand at the time why he can't just get over it. I am better! Why isn't he? Why is he so, so much worse?

He is getting special PTSD eye therapy, which, I am deeply ashamed to report, I think is totally unnecessary. I like to think I don't tell him that, but I'm sure I at least imply it. He relives the night of my suicide attempt again and again. When he looks at me, he says, all he can see is my body on the floor. All he can see is my face that looks like I am dead, although I am alive. I tell him it would be best if he just moves forward, if he stops dwelling on it all the time. I used to have PTSD, and I never got it treated, and look at how great I've done! Just, c'mon, move on!

He cannot move on. My body has become a thing of horror to him, and he plays in his mind each awful scenario over and over.

"You didn't leave *anything*. You didn't leave a note. You hadn't given anyone—including me!—*any* idea you were feeling this way or thinking about this. Did you think about how I would feel if I found you dead, especially since we had an argument earlier? Did you think about the fact that I would be investigated for murder?"

"Well," I say, displaying my incredible level of empathy at the time, "I wouldn't have any of your DNA under my fingernails so it probably wouldn't have gone on for more than a day or so."

That, he says, is not the fucking point.

In August, the day before my birthday, we decide to take a month apart. He asks if he could see me. No, I say. We can communicate by email, and I ask him to send me a nice birthday one.

The next day, I wake up and immediately check my email. Nothing. Throughout the day, I refresh it again and again. I turn on every alert. Nothing. I go into my intensive outpatient, hopeful. I tell myself to wait, that if I wait 20 minutes before I look at my phone, his email will come through.

Nothing.

Nothing.

Nothing.

When I send him an angry email, I get back a beautiful one that makes me cry. But it shouldn't be this hard.

The final straw, though, is when I find out he is texting Carrie. Constantly throughout the day. She is lonely in her new town, he is lonely, and they'd talked a little bit when I was in the hospital, so . . .

Later, I heard they were together.

I can't lie—I was not a huge fan of this. Honestly, I thought I'd never get past it. But then one day I reached out to touch that spiky old anger and it wasn't there. I don't wish 'em luck, but I do wish 'em well. Life isn't simple for anyone.

On the friend front, I have never gotten answers, and won't. I will always wonder what I did, which ways it was or wasn't my fault. I still dream that Carrie and I establish peace, the same way

I dream that my former mother-in-law tells me she has forgiven me. In the Carrie dreams, I apologize for being so unaware of her needs, her emotions. And in return, she tells me she knows she wasn't capable of being there for me, that it was okay for me to need and express that need, and that she, too, is sorry.

CHAPTER 10

So It's Time
to Reconstitute
Your Whole Dang Life

In Which I Do That Exact Thing

I HAVE ALWAYS BEEN BOTH FASCINATED BY AND TERRI-
fied of tornadoes. This a reasonable position to take because they
are awful and unfathomable. They will level a house, leave one
untouched, then level the house on the other side. One of my old
boyfriends had a tornado come through his neighborhood in New
Orleans. There was no damage to his house, save his camping
chair getting sucked off his patio, but the house next door looked
like a dollhouse with the front sheared off. This isn't because they
purposefully skip over certain houses; it's because the main tornado often has smaller tornadic vortices swirling around it, being
dicks. This is just one unpleasant thing about tornadoes.

I'd experienced them before but only from a distance. I remember huddling in an interior hallway with my mother and little
sisters, or underneath desks in elementary school. They show up in
New Orleans and Houston, but not like they do in Hattiesburg,

FUN FACT: ALL TORNADOES HAVE
WERNER HERZOG ACCENTS!

Mississippi, which is part of Dixie Alley,* the second most prolific tornadic area in America. Also, did you know that the United States is far and away the world's leading producer of tornadoes? Truly! We have, like, 1,200 each year right here in the ol' U.S. of A. while everyone else *combined* barely pass 300 in a good year.

I lived in Hattiesburg right out of college, where I was a regional beat reporter for the *Hattiesburg American*, covering every single thing that happened in Lamar County. A *great* deal of positively absurd things happened.

My favorite part of the job was covering a town I'll call Lumpterville, population 1,200. Lumpterville had recently elected a

---

* That name may be changed by the time you read this, but it's Mississippi and Alabama, so I'm not holding my breath.

new mayor, Joey, who was in his 80s and usually wearing his "WORLD'S #1 GRANDPA" hat. He had run on a platform of modernizing Lumpterville. Unfortunately, his modernization efforts consisted mainly of outlawing golf carts on city streets while continuing to drive *his* golf cart, citing mayoral privilege. He wrote an emergency plan that meant, essentially, if there was any kind of emergency, Lumpterville was under martial law with him in command. Perhaps his most unforgivable act was passing the first-ever fireworks laws in the town; before that, you could light off anything, anywhere, any time. The people of Lumpterville chafed under his regime.

Relations between Joey and the town board of aldermen had broken down to the point where someone was always yelling, and those meetings were a hoot. During one especially heated meeting, Joey was trying to block one of the aldermen from shooting off fireworks at his Christmas party, to which he had invited every single person in town—young, old, rich, poor, Black, white—*except* Joey.

During one public comment period, a grisly old man with a cauliflower ear pulled himself slowly to his feet.

"Ah've got somethin' to say!" he yelled. "There is something *wrong*, and there is something *bahhd* in this town, Joe-eh! Why do you think the *good* people, the *Christian* people, of Lumpterville were driven to dump all them deer guts in your drahv-way?"

Apparently, the good Christian people of Lumpterville had indeed gone deer hunting and then decided to express their democratic voice by leaving all the deer-cleanings in Joey's driveway. It was a marvelous time, truly.

One night, maybe four months into the job, I am fast asleep in my bed inside the rickety little carriage house I'm renting for $475 per month. (Eat your heart out, city slickers! But also, my take-home pay is $875 per month before taxes and student loans, so . . .). I am dreaming of literally nothing, of a dark void I am trying to peer in to. All of a sudden, out of it comes a giant, awful face, black but with a red light shining on it, illuminating the cheekbones, forehead, and jawline. His eyes are dark, empty sockets, and he smiles at me and says, "This will be louder than anything," and then . . .

Bam!

Lightning strikes a tree that is maybe 100 feet from my house, and I sit straight up in bed, in the middle of one of the terrifying, amazing storm systems that sweep in from the west and often spawn tornadoes.

I'd fallen asleep to the TV, as I always do. I get one channel with my antenna—WDAM, an NBC affiliate—so I usually stay up and watch *Conan* and then the channel goes off the air at 1:30 a.m. with a patriotic jet-fighter montage (really) and I wake up to loud static.

Tonight, there isn't static. Tonight, there is a full screen of the Doppler radar, showing a big, pulsating red blob with tiny lightning icons flashing, and an off-screen voice saying where they are seeing circulation, noting that now they are seeing a hook echo—the sign a tornado makes on Doppler radar—moving down Hardy Street in the direction of my house.

My carriage house apartment is over a detached garage, maybe 20 or 30 yards from the main house. It was built in the late 1800s or early 1900s and looks like it might fall down just for fun on a Wednesday; there is a definite lean to the whole thing. That night, the whole shack is vibrating. Rain and hail are smacking against the windows, and I have to turn the TV all the way up to hear anything.

I start making the very stupidest plans. Okay. Okay. So, I'm going to find both cats and put them in the dryer. That way, if worse comes to worst and the house *does* collapse, at least they won't be crushed. *Then*, I'm going to put on my bike helmet, wrap myself up in a million blankets, and get underneath my mattress, which is already conveniently located on the floor.

I manage to get both cats in the dryer, to their extreme dismay, and then I put on my helmet, get under the bed, and wait, knowing even as I am doing these things how uneven this fight is. But I have to do something.

I hear a low, rumbling noise. I wait, wait, wait. But the tornado doesn't touch down; it passes over me.

And as the storm lessens, I crawl out from under my mattress, so goddamn triumphant. I have the giddiest feeling in the world. I cheated death! Fuck you, air masses! I feel invincible. The world tried to kill me, but it missed, and here I am, laughing hysterically as I take the cats out of the dryer.

But about an hour later, at 4:30 a.m., my editor, Dan, calls me. No tornadoes touched down in Hattiesburg, but large swaths of the county I cover are leveled. I need to get my ass outta bed, he says, and get to Lumpterville to meet MEMA (the Mississippi Emergency Management Agency), ASAP.

I jump out of bed, pulling on the first pieces of clothing I touch, run out the door to my car, and drive through the still-dark night. I swerve around downed branches; all the streetlights are out. I pull into the Lumpterville Community Center, only then realizing that I'd put on something that featured a plunging neckline and way, way too much boob for any sort of tragic circumstance.

I go in for the briefing with my arms crossed, am downloaded on the worst areas, and head out, stopping at a market along the way to buy a "LUMPTERVILLE BOBCATS" T-shirt to cover my shame.

When I arrive at the trailer park, I am agog. It is triggeringly close to something I had seen a year earlier when I saw the Ninth Ward for the first time after Katrina. In both cases, this had so recently been houses, lives, a neighborhood, and now it was reduced to shards. All the work, all the time, the things these people saved to buy, the baby pictures, the last bowl from their grandmother that they hadn't broken—it was all gone.

In the Ninth Ward, I'd started howling while my friend tried to soothe me. "No," I told her, "you *don't understand*. It's like this all the way to Pascagoula. It's sixty miles of this. It will never get fixed. It will never be okay."

"Well," she said, "it might never be okay, but it will get fixed. It's just going to take a long, long time."

That's a little bit what my life felt like in the fall of 2018. I had no boyfriend, no close friends in Salem, no real job, and no prospects for one. I had just gone through the biggest trauma of my life. Even just telling people about it traumatized them (and me, all over again!), and I had no idea how to explain my year-and-a-half-long absence to everyone else.

I had to build a new friendship circle in town. I had to reconnect with the people I'd drifted away from. I had to get back to being someone who is there for others, who has something to give and wasn't always just taking, taking, taking. I had to figure out the new ways of being alive that would keep me safe and healthy. Most pressingly, I had to learn to walk and reassume the important business of my own ambulation.

These didn't feel like impossible tasks—I mean, most of them seemed doable—but I didn't *feel* like it, especially not at the scale that seemed required. God, I survived this goddamn ordeal, wasn't that *enough*? I now had to fix all the wreckage I caused? It felt exhausting. And although I certainly felt better than I had in a long time, I wasn't necessarily happy. I was just . . . here.

One day, I'm on the phone with Alice. She was my maid of honor at my wedding. We had been so, so close since we were 15, but she was the one who had a baby just a week after Trump was elected. So we'd drifted because she was busy raising a tiny human and I was busy being insane, but it was so good to have her back in my life. I knew then, as I do now, that if I called her, she would be there, and she knows the same.

I tell her the whole horrifying story and then she asks how I'm doing now.

I tell her honestly that I am very glad I'm not dead but that I don't always particularly feel like being alive.

"Well, so—okay, this is something Hannah told me a while back," she says. "You know how it is when you've just gone through a horrible breakup? You wake up and for, like, 30 seconds you don't remember what's happened, and that's the best part of the day. And then you *do* remember, and you're like, well, *fuck*. And then you hate everything.

"You don't want to get out of bed, because it's stupid to get out of bed, because getting out of bed means getting up into the world where this breakup happened. So you're thinking to yourself, *I fucking hate everything! I hate my hallway! I hate that picture! I hate the me in that picture who hasn't yet gone through this breakup! I hate brushing my teeth! I hate my toothbrush! I hate the Crest corporation!* and so on, because everything sucks.

"But . . . you still have to brush your teeth. And you brush your teeth not because you feel like it, or because you're okay. You brush your teeth because you have faith that someday you will *want* to brush your teeth again, that someday not everything will be this exhausting. You brush your teeth even when you don't feel like it so that when you are okay, you still have teeth."

And so I begin to brush my teeth.

There is so, so much about myself that frustrates me, nearly all of which I've listed in this book. But there is one thing, above all, that I take pride in, every day: I am one of the most resilient fuckers you will ever, ever meet. If I survive it, I'm going to get past it. And not only that, I will find my meaning in it. I will figure out why it had to happen and then I will move forward, having turned pain into solidity and strength.

But I have work to do.

Step One: Reestablish Relationships

I worry so much about this one. How do I start these relationships up again when I still feel like such a sucking vacuum of need? How do I tell my friends and family what all has been up with me?

Well, Billy the Therapist says, maybe, just maybe, *I don't need to talk about myself.* I can see how they're doing!

I take a page from my friend Tiqvah. Every morning, while she commutes on the train, she starts texting people and asking how they're doing. She tries to text five to ten people per day, maybe whom she hasn't seen or talked to in a while. I begin doing this, setting up friend dates, asking if people are willing to come visit me at my house because it's still really hard for me to get out.

I call people on the phone. I FaceTime. I send emails and Instagram messages. I reach out to some people in town I'd wanted to get to know better but never had. When I can't walk, I invite people to come visit me at my house, even people I haven't seen in years. To my shock, they come.

I work on remembering everything and following up. How did

your meeting go? Tell me all about that camping trip—it looked gorgeous! Did anything happen with you and that British Tinder man? Last time you weren't liking your job; is it better now?

I draw closer to my family. I've caused them all a lot of trauma. I tell my little sisters that when they're ready to talk about it, I'd like to explain what happened. I'm also able to honestly tell them—backed up by evidence—that it is very, very unlikely to ever happen again. I apologize, and they forgive me.

I let new people into my life. If I meet someone cool when I'm out and about, I save their phone number and then text them and make a date to hang out again. This may sound very normal, but please know that in the chilly, passive-aggressive Pacific Northwest, it is *wild*.

Now, two years later, I don't have a single insanely tight group, but I have good, good friends. Maybe not form-a-commune-level friends, but I am never lonely. I'm a better friend than I used to be because I do not take anyone's love, attention, or time for granted.

Step Two: Get Involved in Things I Care About, Love, and Can Be Accountable To

So there I am, at the Englewood Forest Festival, and what should I spot but the Girl Scouts booth!

I loved Girl Scouts when I was little, especially the crafts. Maybe, just maybe, I could volunteer? They seem to think this is a great idea. Before I know it, I am a troop leader who is beta-testing this book's craft tutorials on seven-year-olds; singing happy, instructive songs about friendship; and talking next to an oak tree about the white fungus that's growing on it.

I love my tiny troop. My main role is coming up with a craft every week, and I go to town. Their favorite is certainly the Shrinky

Dinks. We make rainbows and unicorns and roses and little faces, and I still have some charms that my favorite scout, Beth, made for me.

A bar I enjoy downtown has just moved to a new location. I get to chatting with the owner, whom I've known for years, and say the space is great but they need to do more with the décor. I put together a Pinterest board for them, and they love it. And, hey—they'd been thinking about doing some more events. How would I feel about hosting a trivia night?

It turns out that my best life, the role I was absolutely born to play, was pub trivia host. Mine is called "Questions About Facts," and there is one good prize (a $25 gift certificate to the bar) and then everyone else gets bizarre, upsetting prizes I source from Goodwill or the boxes of childhood items in my mother's basement she's always trying to get me to sort through.

I have my regulars, and I *love* them. I love when new people come. I love getting to see this set of people every week. I love finding the most ridiculous items possible for them. I love collecting trivia questions from people and adding them to a big Google document.

I love that my weeks now have shape.

Step Three: Get a Job

It is time to admit that the dream of being a stay-at-home writer doesn't work for me and is, in fact, not a dream but instead a nightmare.

There are people out there who can work from home, for themselves. I am not and will never be one of them, and admitting this about myself was a big relief.

"You know, you're the only artist I've ever met who longs for a cubicle," Former Husband said once, and he was completely correct. I love a cubicle. Love a coworker. Love asking if you saw *Succession* last night. Love talking about a project together. Love a meeting. Love a fridge with a variety of company-supplied cold LaCroix.

So I start sending out résumé after résumé. My career is a tough one to explain—"Yeah, so for four years I was focused entirely on writing books and long-form journalism and then for 18 months I focused mainly on lying motionless on a couch, spending all my savings on Jimmy John's delivery."

After weeks of nothing, I get a call for an interview. An educational nonprofit in my town is looking for a copywriter. I'm definitely overqualified for it—I think they're looking for someone a couple years out of college—but I leave with an offer and a job description that is pretty darn close to what I can offer.

The first week of my job, I literally cry from happiness at the end of one of the days. Overnight, I'd say I became 50 percent happier. I'm getting to know people, decorating my little area, and thinking about what projects I could do that would be helpful. It sounds small, but it's not. It's fucking huge to have humans in your life who you're accountable to, who you see face-to-face and talk to, who you collaborate with, who you get up in the morning and put your makeup on for.

I love this job, I really do. It is not the sexiest or best-paying job I ever have had, and it's not what I pictured myself doing, but it is *great*. It has taught me something precious: the satisfaction I take at a job is not the title or the specifics of the work I am doing. It comes from the people who I am working with, the connections among us, and what we can do together for a cause we believe in.

My official title, now, is Community Manager. I get to put on my reporter's hat, but I also get to help nurture along a Slack and

Discord community. I build relationships, find out what everyone is up to, connect people, put on panels, and think of new ways to be helpful. I get to work on the fun details of our annual conference—what *is* the best swag under $25, and how shall I customize it? Every day, I have smart, interesting people in my life, and they pay me for it.

✂

Watercolor Valentines for Coworkers and Friends

I've always loved making and giving out Valentines to people because they never see it coming. Someday, I'll reach the level of my darling friend who makes *individual heart cakes with people's names iced on them*, but this craft is also a crowd-pleaser. Bonus points if you grab a bag of fun-sized candy, too, because we all know the best Valentines are the ones that come with candy.

Materials:

- Scissors
- Watercolor paper
- Pencil
- Red and white watercolors, plus something to mix them on (A tiny dish is fine, or if you have a paint tray, great.)
- A cup of water
- Medium-sized paintbrush
- A paper towel
- Sakura Pen-Touch gold pen (optional) (This is *the best* gold paint pen you can have, and it's only $6 or so.)
- Thickish black pen (optional)
- Gold glitter/Mod Podge (optional)

Instructions:

1. Cut your watercolor paper into small rectangles. Usually, those pads come in nice, even sizes, like 9 × 12 inches (22.9 × 30.5cm) or 18 × 24 inches (45.7 × 60.9cm). I usually go for 3 × 4-inch (7.6 × 10.2cm) rectangles, but just cut it down mathematically.

2. In pencil, lightly sketch a heart on each one.

3. You can go for pure red paint, or you can mix it with some white for pink, which is what I usually do.

4. Add a teeny bit of water to mix things together. Remember, you can always add more but never less (unless you want to waste paint).

5. Get your brush wet, and test the water-to-color ratio on scratch paper to assess how watery/transparent you want it.

6. Begin outlining the heart. I like to outline the outside with the color and then use water to spread it around the inside in a wash. If there's too much paint on there, gently press a paper towel directly onto it, and it'll absorb back up.

7. Do all your hearts in one go and then let them dry. You'll be able to tell when they are.

8. Now, some options! The most important thing is putting their name on the heart, so do that. Sometimes I use the gold paint pen for that. If you, too, wish to do this, don't forget to shake it intensely for as long as the packaging tells you to. To get a paint

pen flowing, gently push the tip down repeatedly on scratch paper until the paint comes through. If you're working with a new (to you) pen, be sure to practice a bit on scratch paper until you get a sense of the flow.

9. Another option is doing the name in black pen and then adding little glitter flourishes! As with all calligraphy, the thick part is the downstroke. You can also just do a big first letter and glitter that, *or* do a glitter shine at the edges of the heart.

10. I like to outline the heart itself with glitter, but this isn't important.

11. You don't have to write much on the back, but a little sentence is always great: *Dear X, I'm so glad we get to work together! Hope you and your family have a great Valentine's Day! Love, You.*

12. Get in a little early to put them on people's desks.

✂

Step Four: Start Dating Again

Although I am feeling much, much better, I still feel like an entirely different person than the last time I was single. Then, I was the belle of the ball, a fresh young girl on the cusp of 32! I was bright-eyed and innocent, ready to shyly meet my suitors and be courted. Now, I am an old take-out container. Also, half of my hair has fallen out from trauma, which doesn't help anything.

And yet, the great thing about men is that they never notice anything.

Although I wish I could type that a month after walking away from Sam I found my one true love—an easy, quiet, solid, Sunday sort of love, not rushed or crazy, just easy and steady—that is not what has happened. But I have had a couple great boyfriends and—in a bold, new gamble, for me—have been willing to calmly date people because I like them and they like me.

I do not mistake obsession for love, and I don't require them to go completely crazy over me, although that is still appreciated.

It's been interesting learning how and when to let someone in on what the past couple years have been like. One small relief has been to find that every single person in the world seems to have recently emerged from a uniquely traumatizing period. Or maybe that's just what it is to be human. Everyone has had their hard divorce or lost a parent or a job or a sense of who they were, and it's enough for me to say that I had a really, really bad two years.

Jesus, I hope no future dates ever read this book, though.

Step Five: Walk

Okay, so technically, this is happening concurrently with the others. But it is the scariest of all because if you have not walked for months, it can seem like something only a superhuman can do.

It starts by putting my cast on the ground and slowly shifting my weight back and forth. Soon, I am in a boot, and *clomping, clomp, clomping* around like a pirate who is just so proud of herself.

I do every single physical therapy exercise as often as they tell me. My therapist is shocked; no one, she says, is actually compliant, and I am making incredible progress.

One day, a few weeks ahead of schedule, even, I take off the boot and the therapist laces up this very tight little foot brace. As I take my first steps, I hover my hand above a ballet barre that I can grab if I need it, but I don't need to. I walk to the end. I turn around carefully. I walk back. I do it again. And again. It hurts, but that's not why I'm crying.

That was two years ago, and I think about the fact that I can walk *every single day*. Every day. When I am walking down stairs, I think about placing my foot carefully to protect this precious gift. When I can step over a gap, or off a curb, I just do it, no problem. When I need to pace, I do, Eleanor participating enthusiastically, if not helpfully. It simply does not get old, and I hope it never does.

I still enjoy that I can use my arms. Not as frequently, but certainly more than weekly. It comes to me at surprising times, and every time it does, I also take a moment to feel grateful that, in this moment, my body doesn't hurt. That is a thought that is always, always worth gratitude.

I also find a medical explanation for why I keep breaking bones. It has to do with my joints being too flexible, which means they aren't always in a good alignment for impact. Essentially, my connective tissue is too loosey-goosey, which explains a lot of other health stuff, too. There's not much to be done for it besides joint-strengthening exercises, but understanding the what and why makes it a million times less scary. In one more arena, I have learned how to protect myself.

Step Six: Be Grateful

I do still wonder, all the time, what life is like in the universe where Trump didn't become president. In that world, did I still break so many parts of myself? In that world, were Sam and I happy? In that world, do I still have my friends?

And even as I envy that version of myself—and the version of me before, you know, all this—I also can't really respect her the way I respect myself. That Me, with her soft hands and smooth, quiet mind, was not nearly as resilient or tough as This Me. Because This Me knows precisely what I can endure, and This Me is the one who emerged with sunniness and joy intact.

So perhaps here is the point of it all, my precious plums: bad things happen for good reasons or bad reasons or no reasons at all, to all of us. There is nothing to be done about it except perhaps breathe, abide, and hold on to the faith that no matter how awful today was, you never have to live it again.

You and life have some things in common: you are both more capacious than you seem. Things, both good and bad, change much faster than you imagine they do. You do not know what the future holds. Also, what if you kill yourself, but the next day your worst enemy goes viral and is dunked on by the entire internet? Don't chance it!

The epigraph of this book is from a letter called *Consolation to Helvia* that Stoic philosopher Seneca the Younger sent to his mother after he was exiled to an island: "All your sorrows have been wasted on you if you have not yet learned how to be wretched." This is a lesson I have absorbed *fully*. I have every terminal degree in wretchedness, and now I take comfort in it because I know it is not fatal.

I feel different now, and it's not just the drugs. I do not look for outside things to fill me, and I do not expect happiness, which is really a big ask. I mean, who's happy for more than five minutes at a time?

What I constantly work on is contentment. Having lost almost everything, I feel amused and pleased by all of it. I love the tiny, spherical birds that hop around what I call Bird City, USA (the bird feeder, hummingbird feeder, and a birdbath that are all on my porch, although the birdbath gets little use no matter what I do). Eleanor. My friendships, which I will never again take for granted. My family, who forgave me. My relationship, which is wonderful but will never consume me. My coworkers and my cubicle, my messy kitchen, my neighbors, the Japanese maple in the backyard, reruns of *30 Rock*, finding jars at Goodwill full of painted beans I can give away for trivia prizes—all of it. None of it is owed to me because I tried to throw it all away, and yet it and I are still here.

Afterword

. . . And Now, Here We All Are

WELL. TURNS OUT THAT BEING AN AGORAPHOBIC DEPRES-
sive who has experienced months of being housebound was some
great practice for what lay ahead.

I'm writing this in summer 2020, and America is weird and
unsettling. It's roiling and seems unsustainable, like the world
might tip right over.

When the pandemic quaratine started, all the structures I'd set
up to keep myself healthy disappeared in a single week. Once
again, it was just me by myself in the house, wondering how to get
through the day. But unlike the last time I was trapped in my
house, this time everyone in the world was doing it, too. Sorry,
everyone.

The pandemic and resulting quarantine period has scraped us
all bare and revealed so many things, good and bad. It's made me
realize, again and again, how tender we all are. How we need one
another, and when we can't be together, things begin to break
down. There are so many overlapping crises right now, it's hard to

pick one to focus on. But I find myself, again and again, thinking of all the people who feel sad and alone, who are losing hope and are sure nothing will ever be okay.

And maybe it won't be! Who knows? You're the one reading this in the future. But for now, the only option is to abide, snatch joy where I can, and tell myself every day that passes is a day we're closer to a vaccine.

That is a silver lining. The gold lining, for me, is that I now know every neighbor on my block. We get together and drink wine in backyards, and I chat with their kids during pauses in water balloon fights. I know, in an emergency, that I can hop on the group text and someone will be there to help. We have all made the others promise they'll never move away. This is a new kind of safety.

We get together for craft nights on picnic tables that Neighbor Heather sets up on her patio. The most recent one was rock painting; I made six to hide in the park nearby. I was hoping to do more origami with Sean, my 10-year-old neighbor and fellow crafter. The week before, I'd taught him how to make the sonobe unit, bringing him one of mine so he could deconstruct it and learn how the pieces fit together, which he was truly jazzed about.

That night, I bring strips to make lucky paper stars.

"Hey, Sean," I say, holding up a little-bitty star. "Have you seen these before? Do you want to know how to make them?"

He scrunches up his face.

"Nah," he says. "Stars aren't cool, honestly."

I laugh as his mother scolds him for being rude, and I go back to painting my rock.

While it's drying, I grab the strips and my fingers move reflexively.

"Oh my God, that's so cute!" Gabbie says, and I tell her she can have as many stars as she wants, forever.

I look around and feel so, so grateful for the friends around me, these people to care for, the fragile, precious gift of togetherness. The chosen family we make.

I cannot believe how wildly lucky I am to be on that exact patio, with these people, on a beautiful summer night, feeling safe and content as tiny paper stars emerge and fall from my hands.

Acknowledgments

I owe a lot of people a lot of gratitude. Also, I know there is some-one major that I'm leaving out and I cannot for the life of me fig-ure out who it is, and if it is you, I'm so, so sorry.

First and foremost, thanks to my editor, Michelle Howry, whose insight, vision, and encouragement took this from a sad little lump into something I actually like. An equal thank-you is due to Brooke Jackson-Glidden, who not only was an incredible editor but also one of the people who saw me through the dark-ness. Thank you to Brandi Bowles, who for 10 years has been someone I trust above all others. Thank you to Dana Spector for being a voice of reason and encouragement.

Thank you also to the team at Putnam: First, Ashley Di Dio, who is so patient, careful, and kind. Thank you to Christy Wagner for her incredibly sharp eye, plus Andrea St. Aubin, Maija Baldauf, Meredith Dros, Ashley Tucker, and Bill Peabody. Thank you to Ashley McClay, Brennin Cummings, Alexis Welby, and Kristen Bianco for helping me get the word out; and Monica Cordova, Anthony Ramondo, and Philip Pascuzzo for making it so beauti-ful inside and out. Thank you to Ivan Held and Sally Kim for giv-ing me this opportunity.

ACKNOWLEDGMENTS

Thank you to the places in Salem that were so welcoming, especially everyone at f/Stop and Brown's Towne Lounge.

I am so very grateful to all the people in the mental health field who helped me during the worst period of my life—they and their colleagues do wrenching, emotional work for lots of people who are in very bad shape, and they don't get to see us once we're okay.

Thanks to Stephen Yamada and Thomas Richards for being so kind, flexible, and supportive throughout this process. You are both such mensches.

Thank you to everyone who read this, *especially* early on— Henrietta Wildsmith, Sarah Moore, Kate Schroeder, Meredith Haggerty, Dr. Brian Esparza, Lizzie Post, Tiqvah Pearl, Jessica Lyness, Bronte Brooke, and my beloved Bryan Jacobs.

An absolutely enormous heap of gratitude goes to my mom, Barbara, who was and is such a trooper, and to all my family—my dad, Joel; my sisters, Olivia and Elizabeth—for unconditional love and support, for forgiving me, and for not feeling sorry for me.

Finally, thank you to Joe, for believing so hard in this, and me.

About the Author

Kelly Williams Brown is a writer who lives in Oregon with a giant dog named Eleanor. In the past, she has written other books, along with many magazine and newspaper articles. She's actually feeling pretty good these days.